I Thought He Was Dead

I Thought He Was Dead

A Spiritual Memoir

Ralph Benmergui

Published by James Street North Books
an imprint of Wolsak and Wynn Publishers
280 James Street North
Hamilton, ON L8R 2L3
www.wolsakandwynn.ca

Publisher and Editor: Noelle Allen | Copy editor: Andrew Wilmot
Cover and interior design: Jennifer Rawlinson
Cover images: Beach Walk, Adam Goldberg Photography; microphone and chair vector illustration, jemastock
Author photograph: Chelsea Smith, Vintage Chic Portrait
Typeset in Minion and Six Hands
Printed by Brant Service Press Ltd., Brantford, Canada

Printed on certified 100% post-consumer Rolland Enviro Paper.

10 9 8 7 6 5 4 3 2 1

The publisher gratefully acknowledges the support of the Ontario Arts Council, the Canada Council for the Arts and the Government of Canada.

Library and Archives Canada Cataloguing in Publication

Title: I thought he was dead / Ralph Benmergui.
Names: Benmergui, Ralph, author.
Identifiers: Canadiana 20210257601 | ISBN 9781989496336 (softcover)
Subjects: LCSH: Benmergui, Ralph. | LCSH: Television personalities—Canada—Biography. | LCSH: Radio personalities—Canada—Biography. | LCSH: Sephardim—Canada—Biography. | LCSH: Old age. | LCGFT: Autobiographies.
Classification: LCC PN1992.4.B46 A3 2021 | DDC 791.4502/8092—dc23

*For my boys, Jonah, Chas, Emmanuel and Isaiah, and to
Cortney, my beloved wife, who has filled my heart with love*

*For my father, Mair Soto Benmergui
May his memory be a blessing*

Contents

Stents, Radiation and the
   Dawn of Mortality: A Leaf Falls   1

What Doesn't Kill Ya   9

Goodbye, Papa   15

The Palace of Loneliness   23

What's That on My Hand   27

That's Not the Way to Wash a Boy!   43

Ralph Becomes Raphael   55

Tuesday Is Seniors' Discount Day   75

When You Work You Always Have Tomorrow   83

Extra, Extra, Read All About It!   97

Friday Night with Ralph Benmergui   117

Jump! You'll Grow Wings on the Way Down   127

Who's Ralph Benmergui? Get Me Ralph Benmergui   133

Old and Improved   143

Politics, Jazz and *Friday Night* 2.0   149

Take Your Time and Let Us Know   175

Changing the Channel   177

I'm Spiritual – Not Religious   197

Love – To Hold Dear   205

Into the Woods   213

Take Two Teaspoons of Agape and
  Call ME in the Morning   221

Love Me, Love Me Not   225

Eldering: The Way Forward   233

The Harvest   259

From Success to Significance   261

What's the Plan?   267

Not That Kind of Rabbi   273

Do Not Cast Me Off in Old Age;
  When My Strength Fails, Do Not Forsake Me!   283

Epilogue   287

Stents, Radiation and the Dawn of Mortality: A Leaf Falls

It was 5:15 a.m. and the dead of winter. As usual I had dressed in the dark, tiptoed downstairs and was on my way to work as a jazz radio morning show host. I opened the front door, and as the first blast of winter air filled my lungs, I felt what I can best describe as a clutching scream of sorrow in my chest. Was this anxiety? I'd had anxiety attacks in my early twenties. Now, at fifty-four, was this an encore?

I had been through a divorce, remarried and now had two teenagers living with me half the time, along with two more boys under three tucked away upstairs. I took a second breath, and again felt that clutch at my throat, my chest and my upper back. I thought about turning around and going right back inside, into the warmth of my house, but when you host a daily morning show you can't just call at the last minute and tell them you're not quite up to it today. If you do, the last question you'll be asked is whether you're all right. I went to work.

As days passed, I felt as if my batteries were wearing out. I was tired – profoundly so. Eventually I went to see my doctor. A note on his door said the office was temporarily closed. I groaned. Now I would have to go to the walk-in clinic. I didn't have time for this crap. Still, I went.

Strange thing about doctors: You're supposed to be on time, they're supposed to listen to you and every other patient. Instead, you sit and wait, wondering what the person sitting across from you in the reception area has. Eventually you are called, but only so that you can wait even longer. This time alone, surrounded by anatomy charts and tongue depressors. Finally, the wait is over, the doctor enters.

This practitioner was cold, aloof. He held himself in a way that said, Ignore this clinic, I'm better than this. He stared at his sheet and asked what brought me in. "Well," I replied, "my doctor doesn't seem to be around so I came here."

"Who is your doctor?" he asked. I told him the name. "Oh, him. He's dead."

I was shocked, both at the news and at how remarkably insensitive this man had been in telling me. I liked my now-dead doctor; he was a kind, casual practitioner. He would enter the waiting room with a flourish and call your name with a "Come on down" sense of enthusiasm. His office was piled high with papers, the walls covered with golf memorabilia he had collected over so many afternoons when he had closed the office early and hit the greens. He usually had a Diet Coke in hand. I found out later, by returning to his office and speaking to his loyal and loving receptionist, that he had died alone on his couch from insulin shock. Turns out he'd been severely diabetic.

Deeply distracted, I sat staring at this other healer, the kind that, for whatever reason, seemed to leave their heart outside the examination room. I proceeded to tell him about my chest pains.

"Does cold air affect you more?"

"Yes, it does," I replied.

"Are you running out of breath after climbing stairs?"

Much as I didn't want to admit it, that too was correct.

"You're describing angina," he said. "I can't help you. But I can refer you to a cardiologist."

I thanked him and left.

My doctor was dead, I was in trouble and life – my life – was changing. It all seemed so fragile. I walked up the street and back to my house, my family, my job.

The cardiologist was kind. I sensed that he knew me from my radio work, something that I find often leads to a certain generosity from which most patients don't benefit. It was a way of saying thank you for keeping me company, if only as a disembodied voice.

With the niceties out of the way, the diagnostics began. The progression of the symptoms was, by the look on his face, profound. I failed the stress test. I failed most of the tests. I had begun the journey across the bridge from a person of interest, as they say in the crime world, to a prime suspect. Meanwhile I stayed on the air, doing my morning shift from six to ten every morning, five days a week. I was unhappy and scared. It seemed like I was living someone else's life. How could this be? I had just started a second family and now I felt like I was letting everybody down.

Like most men I know, I had been raised to provide, to satisfy a primal imperative as an urbanized hunter-gatherer – granted, a very winded hunter-gatherer. Finally, after excusing myself from almost all my household chores and lying on the couch, trying to keep my breathing shallow so as not to rouse the angina beast, my wife had had enough. She was scared, and that fear came out as anger.

I felt I knew what she was thinking: "How could you do this to me, leave me with these children to raise? I should have known. What was I thinking, marrying an old(er) man?"

She took me to the hospital where my cardiologist checked my vitals and pronounced, "You have to go to a hospital across town, right now. They will be waiting for you. You're getting an angiogram so that they can look inside and see what's happening." I gathered up my car keys and looked into the very worried eyes of my wife, who couldn't decide whether to comfort me or give me a stern lecture about taking lousy care of myself. The doctor, seeing the keys in my hand, stopped me as I shuffled toward the door.

"You're not thinking of driving, are you?"

"Yes," I muttered. "It's the only time the pain goes away."

"If you insist on driving, I'm going to have to call the police." He turned to my wife. "Under no circumstances is he to drive." She took my keys.

Three hours later, I was on a table, catheter inserted through my wrist and straight into my heart, an inky dye being injected into my clogged arteries. I was awake and watching the screen. The blockages were clearly visible. The doctor made that sound that contractors make when renovating a kitchen. You know, where they cut out a piece of drywall and look at your electrical wiring and go, "Oooh, no, yeah, mmm." At this point he left.

A second doctor appeared. This one, I was told, was proficient in the art of passing drug-alluded stents – little tubes, really – through the body and lodging them in place so that the plaque-filled dam could burst. When he achieved that small miracle, the arterial tree that runs through my heart came back to full flower. I felt the pressure build in my chest, and then relief. It was over. I was told that both arteries were 95 percent blocked. One, the LAD, or the "widow-maker" as they call it, was within days, if not hours, of bringing on a massive heart attack.

At that moment my world view began to change. I went from what others described as a young fifty-ish broadcast personality to a man with heart disease, two chaotic teenagers and two little boys. This was my first inkling that life, indeed, is not a rehearsal. It ended my delusion that dying was something that other people did. It ended my self-sustaining myth that I was in no way finished with what I had to do here, and because of that my number, quite simply, could not be up.

It's quite spectacular, really, how we can wake up every morning and convince ourselves that others may die, indeed will die, but that we are not part of the conversation. If you ask me, I'll say, well of course I'll die. But deep down, I feel that if I carry that cold hard stone around with me in any real way, then meaning and purpose will simply fade.

All these existential thoughts, lovely as they may be, were rudely interrupted when the stents that had been working fine, at least for the first six months, started acting up. I had a restenosis, as they call it, where the artery for the crucial one, the widow-maker, had over-healed, building a new blockage. It was back to the hospital then, where a third stent was inserted.

During the next while, I found myself in a rehab centre as part of the healing regimen offered by the hospital. I was suddenly surrounded by dozens of people with heart disease. At least half also had diabetes. I started the program with a stress test, where you walk on a treadmill with a plastic mask strapped to your head and a tube between your teeth attached to a monitoring device of some kind. I stood there on a treadmill feeling awkward, like I was on a space station a la Stanley Kubrick's *2001: A Space Odyssey.*

I was snapped back to earth by the cardiologist, who had positioned herself in front of a bank of machines and asked without looking up, "Before we begin, any questions?"

"Yes." I lifted the mask from my mouth. "Why me? I mean, no offense, but I don't look like any of those men in the waiting room. They're big and old and tired looking."

Her back was still to me as she checked the machines I was attached to. "Tell me about your family heart history," she said.

I began to rattle off all the cardiac "events" in my family's history. The list was impressive: heart attack, stroke, bypass, angina. She stopped me somewhere in the middle of this depressing litany of broken hearts.

"It's mostly genetic," she told me. I was immediately comforted. In fact, I was downright brimming with a newfound arrogance. This had nothing to do with getting older, or years of stress, smoke and ambition. This was fated, and as such there was little to learn from it. It was in my genes, I thought, as if my genes belonged to some other fool and not me.

Part of the vulnerability that comes before a diagnosis is some portion of guilt. What did I do? What didn't I do? Sometimes when sharing news with friends about someone's grave illness or death, there emerges a stream of conversation that revolves around what they, the afflicted one, did wrong. Implied in that is the idea that we deserve our fates. I drank, I smoked, I definitely ate too much pizza. If I had just done it "right," I wouldn't have failed. I wouldn't have to die.

The inference is that death is for others; that a moral and good life, including, apparently, a rather healthy portion of dark green leafy produce, will save me from their end. Regardless of the facts, and they are irrefutable, we dance into the night certain that if we just get the footwork right the sun will rise yet again.

Having just become a man with little drug-coated tubes in my arteries, it was incumbent on me to not fail. I had to eat right, take lots of daily meds and above all, keep moving. Hell, they even wanted me to jog. When I see people jogging, I find it annoying. Especially the ones that carry on a full conversation with their running partner as they motor along, as if to say, "I'm not even winded – gasping is for wimps."

So, in spite of my rehab coach's best intentions, I knew this jogging thing wasn't in the cards. We settled on a gentler path – walking, quickly, and a lot. At first, we did this on an indoor track at the rehab facility. I started out doing inner fist pumps as I lapped my fellow walkers. Eventually I realized the ridiculousness of my achievement, unclenched my inner fist and just concentrated on getting my times down, my humility up and my heart rate steady.

What Doesn't Kill Ya

So here I was, a fifty-four-year-old man with heart disease. I can't deny that I felt a certain sadness when I began to process what I had just been through. It was as if Death itself had suddenly and without warning given me a little shake, saying, "Hi there, just checking in with you. That could have been it, you know. If I hadn't tipped you off with the angina thing you would have been another one of those guys who just does a face plant on the sidewalk on an otherwise lovely day. You'd have been mine before you hit the ground."

Odd as it may sound, there is something comforting in that face-plant thing. No long slow battle with some hideous ailment, no burden to family and friends and, most importantly, no suffering. That is what we fear most – the suffering. But, as concentration camp survivor Dr. Viktor Frankl said: "If there is a

9

meaning in life at all, then there must be a meaning in suffering. Suffering is an ineradicable part of life, even as fate and death. Without suffering and death, human life cannot be complete."

If that is true, then why do we compound our suffering by taking such great efforts to avoid it? Are we so driven to seek pleasure that we learn nothing from our pain? I have always thought that the only real teacher in my life has been pain. What pushes me forward is not the desire-driven moments of escape and fleeting euphoria – those moments are small, sweet fruits; it is the pain. If I bring myself into a relationship with pain, breathe through it and transform my anxious fear of it so that I am available to it – that pain sears, scars and focuses me. When I am wounded, I'm given the opportunity to tend to that wound, and in that caring bring forth a loving attitude toward myself and an unfolding compassion for others.

Stephen Jenkinson, author of *Die Wise*, spent decades in palliative care – or as he calls it, the death industry. He views suffering as a product of our wanting, and the pain we feel when relief is denied. "Suffering . . . comes from an unwillingness in this culture to recognize how on the take we have been through the entire course of our lives here, how willing and able we are to wring from the world all we desire and require from it, as if that were the reason the world is here at all."

Jenkinson sees the bitterness some encounter as they enter into their dying this way: "So many people I worked with died with the grudge of *being owed something* by life that they now won't live to collect on. Their deaths were a theft and betrayal."

In thinking of my own demise, I sometimes get the nagging feeling that I will waste my last breath feeling hard done by. Feeling really sorry for myself. Why me? I wasn't finished.

I have things I want to say, do, feel. There have to be a lot more awful people who should go before me. But let's not get ahead of ourselves.

For now, there was something strangely comforting in identifying myself as someone with heart disease. Perhaps I could jump the bitter-last-days queue. Just go about my business and then just drop. A clutch of the left arm, heart attack and . . . out. But I still needed time to digest all this new and not-so-wonderful information. I felt quite secretive about my new condition. I only told certain people, and I certainly wasn't going online to share my trials and tribulations with "friends" and "followers." That would signal that I was headed for the sidelines, moving to the back of the sidewalk as the parade passed me by. I had already had a taste of that in my forties with back surgery. I had been stricken with sciatic pain, a powerful searing pain like a toothache that travels from the lower spine, down the back of the leg and into the foot. While I suffered from this, I was still walking to the nearest transit stop and slowly making my way to the CBC broadcast studios; there I had to stand on set and host a one-hour town hall talk show five days a week. I walked to the train very slowly as people thirty years older breezed past me. Every step was excruciating.

Through that pain I gained humility. I had typically ignored stories about people with lasting injuries, but now I cried to think of these poor people who just happened to be in the wrong place at the wrong time, often described in newscasts as having sustained serious but non-life-threatening injuries. Perhaps they'd been looking left when a car, approaching from the right, came out of nowhere and changed their lives forever. My heart went out to them as I started to get an inkling of how so many people suffer chronic pain without respite.

You see, every passing malady confronts the false sense of entitlement we all have, which Jenkinson writes about in *Die Wise*. We wrap ourselves in the nostalgic fog of the ego, the urge to stay the same, forever and always. Our hair never turns grey; our clothes stay tight to the body. We yearn not for wisdom but for a kind of vitality that reassures us that we still have utility; that someone will need us, pay us, hear us. Like Tom Cruise or Jennifer Aniston in their fifties, grabbing you by the voyeuristic eyeballs and challenging you to think of them as anything other than sexy twenty-six-year-olds.

In a world where so much is commodified, we become a demographic – in this case one that apparently ambles to the drugstore for the seniors' discounts. Or, if the fifty-five-plus magazines are to be believed, we spend our days travelling the world, hang-gliding into our late seventies and getting a little "work" done on our bodies. We must prove that we are still vital, active and – most importantly – buying stuff. When you're thirty-seven, you still have at least four more car purchases ahead of you. By sixty-seven, you're looking for a vehicle that has some lumbar support and, the good Lord willing, heated seats.

I've had my brush with mortality, my wake-up call. But let's tap on the brakes here. I was still in my mid-fifties, with a second family that included two new boys under four. I had been blessed through my working life with many meaningful opportunities. Still, I was feeling the need to retreat from parts of that life.

I had been a broadcaster and a public figure for a long time, and some of it had been hard. I was aware when someone would walk by and whisper my name, impressed not necessarily by me but by the fact that I was from the land of television. I, like many of my colleagues, always felt a bit awkward about that. Sometimes a person would stand in front of me, looking me over like a department store mannequin, and say to their friend, "Do you know this guy? Wait, don't tell me your name. You're on TV. It's one of those funny names, Brent, Brent-something."

"No, Ben! It's Ben-something," her friend would pipe in. I have to tell you, these folks must be angels sent down to poke your ego in the eye. Yet, I had seen so much beauty, interviewed so many fascinating people and reaped the comforting rewards that come with being a public person in Canada. But now, with what I had been through, a door had been opened – this door had been opened before in my life, I just hadn't walked through.

The lessons of life are only heard when we are ready to listen.

Goodbye, Papa

I remember the day, in my early thirties, when I got the phone call that my entire family had been anticipating. After three years of major and minor strokes, my father was in the hospital again. I had gone to visit him the day before and just looked at him, lying there, curled up on the gurney. He was so much smaller than I wanted to remember him as being. He could no longer form words, but upon seeing my two young boys, one just a year old, crawling on the bed beside him, he managed a small soft sound and a weak smile.

He was leaving us, but I had no ability to sit with that. I had never really appreciated my father. I wanted him to be tougher. To fight back at all the ignorance and condescension he had lived with as a nursing assistant, shuttling people around the hospital for X-rays. Cleaning up after them. Enduring constant

"Where are you from?" questions because of the darker colour of his skin and his obvious Spanish accent. I had wanted him to stand up to my mother when she got mad. But that was not his way. He preferred to avoid confrontations.

On the way home that day, my first wife gently said, "He's not long for this world. He's going." I'd shrugged it off. I had often claimed that I was okay with death, and sometimes encouraged people to appreciate the trail of love that so many of us leave behind rather than dwell on their passing. But this time I didn't want to hear what I myself had professed. The next night, late in the evening, the phone rang. I answered, and a member of the hospital staff told me that my father had just died. Not like the storybook says, with his loving family around him, but alone, in a hospital room, in the dark.

It's wonderfully strange what we remember sometimes. Of all the time we had together, I found myself plucking out this one moment. I was five, and we lived in social housing in a place called Regent Park, in the east end of Toronto. For the record, no good comes of grouping together people who are either newly arrived or generationally poor, mixing in with them a good dollop of stigma and hopelessness. The result is a toxic social stew. Luckily, as social planning goes, the ideas that spawned that particular experiment have mostly faded. Nonetheless, there we were in the middle of this really bad idea, trying to get by and get out.

Coming from Morocco, the game of hockey was not in our cultural wheelhouse. One day I was standing with my father outside of our cream-coloured townhouse and he gave me something. Now my father, like me, was no handyman, but he had nailed together a wooden shaft and blade that resembled a hockey stick. I don't remember how long that stick lasted but the gift stays in my heart. This man, lost in a new world where all rules had been changed, had found some wood and made me a stick so that I could try and fit in even though he could not. I can only imagine that he had seen other kids playing hockey and perhaps me standing there, his youngest, only watching. Now, thirty years later, that act of kindness percolated up in my heart.

My father was a good man, and I have always regretted not having spent the kind of time with him that he truly deserved, but I did absorb some of his wisdom. He always taught me that each person is to be taken as they are. We are all people, and the thing to do is to pay attention to the person right in front of you.

If you ask a deeply diverse group of people to move to another part of the room if they think of themselves as shy, or the youngest, or the class clown, all their preconceived barriers dissolve. They did that once, on a Nordic television program, and it brought tears to my eyes. These people all assumed that they were of a certain group, as it were – truckers, academics, artists, lefties, righties – but once asked to stand together not according to their professions, skin colour or country of origin but rather if they were stepfathers or took daily medication or had been the class clown they became what we all really are: human beings. My father believed in that, even though he identified strongly as Jewish, Moroccan and Spanish, in that order. He knew we were above all human.

Growing up, this was not wisdom shared equally among my community. Instead, there was a defensive kind of exceptionalism. A hollow assertion that we were just better – better than the horrible things they had done and said to us for millennia. Our mothers cooked better food, our religious services were more meaningful and appropriate. Luckily for me, these messages missed their mark.

I still long for my dad and, as the father of four children, two now well into adulthood and two still quite young, often try to bargain with God so that I might have enough time to watch them all grow into men. The negotiations go something like this: "God, if you let me stay for another twenty years, I can make sure that they're okay. I'll settle for fifteen, but twenty would be nice, keep me in good health till then." But in truth, I don't believe in a transactional God who grants wishes. That's a Santa Claus–God. I'm just trying to say that wanting a long life isn't really about me; it's about my boys, my grandchildren, my wife, all those who I love so deeply.

As I wrote these reflections on my father, I received a shock. A dear soul, a man in his forties with a warm and loving way about him, had died suddenly. He'd always had a smile for everyone, and deep generosity. He had a caring and loving wife and a little girl. He, by his own admission, was out of shape, but he wanted to change that. One night while he was out running, his heart seized up. He had a massive heart attack and died later in hospital. Just like that. In the middle of his life. With a little girl waiting for him at home.

At times like this it can seem that our lives are part of some cosmic mockery. A cursory glance at his social media profile feels like an exercise in futility. Marketing: Developing and executing marketing and communication strategies that deliver results. Specialties: Experiential Marketing, Social Media Strategy and Execution, Search Engine Optimization, PR and Strategic Communications.

Who needs such skills if it is all for naught? "Here, have a life for a little while, and oh, by the way, I'll take it from you whenever, for no great reason and regardless of your best – or worst for that matter – intentions." There is no logic upon which we can hang our threads of hope.

What the hell did he do to deserve this? He was a good man, a young man with a loving child and wife. He was a servant of his community. Wha'd you kill him for? There are plenty of better candidates for the injustice of an early death.

But what if we let go and find a different lens through which we view our demise? As Jenkinson writes in *Die Wise*: "Life, as I said earlier, is not 'the human life span.' Life is by every measure a bigger thing, a more devout and devotion-inspiring thing, a truer thing, than the human life span. Life is that of which the human life span, for a while, partakes." Jenkinson continues: "Our secular humanist religions will not tolerate it, but let us be humble on this point: *Life is not a human thing.* It is what gives us the opportunity to be human. It is not the stage upon which we play out our humanity or our lack of it, though merely players we surely are. It is the play. And the play's the thing."

This notion that our life is not "life" itself but that the human moment is a shooting star of indeterminate luminosity does not sit well when news arrives that a decent, worthy fellow fell to the ground and died without closure. It seems cruel to talk of the eternity of the soul when the press of human flesh and that warmth it can bring have disappeared. Did I not fashion this life to make things better for others?

My father never had fulfilling work after he came to Canada. It was hard to see him put on good clothes every day, drive my mother to work, and then slip out of his suit and don the scrubs of an orderly. He was a proud man and that job was one of the few that he felt he could get in a new country, with four children to feed. He did try – he made a brief escape into the world of property management. Aced the test, found a job, then the company went under and no one else was willing to give a man in his fifties another chance. But truth be told, he wasn't much of risk-taker. He returned to the work he knew, where, as a union man, he earned a decent wage. Once again he fell into a daily routine: arriving at work, changing into hospital-issued greens and helping patients as best he could. He found his solace in other places, in synagogue and community life. He served once as synagogue president, and always took the same seat for services in the sanctuary. There he had comfort and found a measure of dignity.

I was able to attend my father's retirement party at the hospital where he worked. His co-workers and a few of his family were in attendance. I was visiting from Winnipeg, where I was living at the time, and stayed with my mother-in-law in suburban Toronto. That night, after the retirement party, I got the phone call – my father had suffered a massive stroke.

I rushed to the hospital. I'm still not quite sure if he had died and was resuscitated, but I knew that he would never be the same again. His official retirement was three days away. He would be confined to a wheelchair for three years, till his passing. His bags were packed for a journey with my mother to see relatives in Venezuela; instead he embarked on a journey into debilitation and decline. In essence, my father never got to grow old, to walk into the forest of his life, as the Hindus say. So one night, three years after his retirement, I got another call. He was dead.

No great cry left my throat. This wasn't the movies, and

the grief would manifest slowly over many years, catching me by surprise when it did. That night I quietly got dressed and headed to the hospital, alone, to wait for the Jewish community's burial society members to arrive. My brothers lived out of town. My sister would follow later. I entered the room and saw my father there.

I went up to him and stroked his forehead. Some parts of him were warm; some, like his hands, had already gone cold. Then I looked into his eyes. They had gone from clear to hooded, a milky white residue forming. I had never seen a dead person before. We hide the dead in our culture until we can dress them up in some strange mockery of life. When I looked into those eyes, I realized that my father was no longer there. Where he was, I could never pretend to explain or know. Simply, I was looking at a shell, what Ram Dass calls a "spacesuit" that we are given to inhabit this life, this exploration.

I came to two realizations through this experience. One, that mystery deserves a place of honour in our lives. Not all is rational and, sad as it may be, the result of not respecting that path is that we are reduced to a collection of body parts to be inventoried and maintained like some mid-sized sedan. And two, that essence, that spark that animates our lives, was no longer behind those eyes. His soul had departed; only his body remained, and it would now begin to dissolve.

I believed strongly, at that moment and from then on, that we have souls. It is the universal embodied in the particular. Our soul connects us to each other, and our soul's work is the task of our lifetimes. To refine the soul is to deepen the meaning and connection that our everyday lives present to us. Good deeds make our souls shine brighter.

Our sense of self-worth, however, cannot be content with

these answers. In his book *This Is Real and You Are Completely Unprepared*, Rabbi Alan Lew writes:

> Against the encroachment of nothingness, we fill our lives with stuff. Against the ultimate negation, we strive for success. Against the hard information that we came from nothing and end there as well, against the resulting suspicion that we might, in fact, be nothing all the while, we struggle mightily to construct an identity, but we're never quite persuaded by it. Some deep instinct keeps whispering to us that it isn't real, and the walls keep falling down, and then the city finally collapses, and the identity we have been laboring so desperately to shore up collapses along with it.

This life is fragile; this life is not a rehearsal. What my father had spent a lifetime waiting for, what so many of us wait for, is release from who we think we must be. What we lose so often is who we really are.

The Palace of Loneliness

Years ago, a close friend of mine embarked on a pilgrimage. He went to the small town in Sicily that his parents were from. One morning, as he sat at a local café, luxuriating in the island sunshine and sipping an espresso, he saw the child of one of his cousins who still lived in town walking down the narrow, ancient street. The child saw an old man sitting in front of his apartment. The boy stopped, not just to say hello but also to talk. They stayed that way, chatting back and forth for a good ten minutes before the boy took his leave, tossing a *ciao* over his shoulder at the smiling gentleman. My friend was struck by what he witnessed. Mostly because he had never seen such a scene play out organically back home. We, I think, have lost so much.

For many, aging is accompanied by the terrifying notion of being warehoused, pining for a visit not from someone paid to be near you but from someone you love. I came face to face with this when I had to fulfil chaplaincy hours while completing my training in Hashpa'ah, Jewish Spiritual Direction, which is a path within rabbinical studies. I could have worked these hours at a local hospital or even a hospice centre, but I chose a local, mostly Jewish retirement home. I looked forward to the experience; I felt I had a chance to be useful to people in their late sixties, seventies and beyond. The facility was well maintained and the staff seemed content. My job was to knock on people's doors as I went up and down the hall of the long-term area, introduce myself and see if they wanted to have a chat. Easy, I thought.

Not so much.

I was terrified as I entered their rooms. These people had not asked to see me. They were often sitting quietly or with the TV going like an endless, soulless companion in the background. The loneliness that often filled these rooms was thick, sorrowful and palpable. This was not the end result of a life of community and connection – this was much smaller than that.

As I walked through those doorways, I often felt that the people I was visiting allowed me in mostly because they had abdicated the private space that allows us to decide who comes and goes in our lives. Nurses, personal support workers (PSWs), specialists, orderlies with food trays – they came and went mostly devoid of love or malice.

As time went on, I learned to sit with these elders as they unspooled bits of their lives. One day I entered the room of a man I had not met before. The walls were covered with pictures of his family: his wife in a classic posed portrait that she must have sat for decades earlier; the children and their offspring, mostly Orthodox, as was obvious by their clothing. Looking around the crowded room, I noticed many religious artifacts arranged around his sleeping area, almost like a moat in their positioning. His head was covered by a yarmulke, well worn, black and secured by hairpins. His back was curved and his gaze was pointed downward. He had some difficulty moving his head from side to side. Sitting across from him in an oversized leatherette chair was a personal care worker, a small Filipino man absent-mindedly scrolling through his phone. He left as I entered.

The old man had obvious and severe tremors in his right hand, which, occasionally as we talked, shook. He was intrigued by my last name. "Benmergui. That's a Sephardic name. Where are you from?" he said, his voice soft and quivering.

"I'm Moroccan," I replied. I have grown accustomed to explaining my origins. It was clear with a last name like mine that I wasn't from eastern Europe-Ashkenazi. The *Fiddler on the Roof* Jews, as I would sometimes call them when explaining the difference to non-Jewish friends.

After establishing my Jewish credentials, we entered a different space. A deep sorrow hung about this frail old man. As we spoke, it became clear that he was tortured by regret. His wife had died, he told me, and he felt responsible for her death. He hadn't done enough to save her. He repeated that phrase several times, his voice growing thick with emotion. Without saying it explicitly, I knew he was telling me that she had committed suicide. But what mattered most to me was that this man was living his life in a crushing purgatory and did not feel that God was with him.

I asked, "Where is God in all this?" Knowing that he was a religious man, I was curious to hear what he would say.

"God has turned his face away from me. He has abandoned me," he blurted out as he began to cry, his breathing becoming laboured. His hand was shaking violently now.

As the room darkened around us, the care worker returned from his break. He looked at his client, then at me. Not knowing what had transpired, he returned to his seat. He did not comfort the man but also did not interfere with our conversation. The space, I guess, seemed safe.

Slowly, after a few minutes, the old man's breathing returned to normal and the sobbing subsided. We left the conversation about his wife, and he seemed lighter in a way to have unburdened himself. I'm not sure if he regularly purged these feelings of guilt and regret, but at least in this instance, he seemed relieved. I asked him who the people were on the wall. His sons, their families. The sons, he said, would visit on alternating weekends. In between it was apparent he would sit in a chair beside his bed, looking down, saying little. He was surrounded by a life once lived, waiting for the end. Was every day like this? No – I did see him several more times, and he seemed less pained. But that first encounter will stay with me forever.

I don't believe it when people say they have no regrets. To have no regrets is to have not felt your life. We are painfully imperfect. Regret is the child of effort gone wrong. My fear, and the fear of many I have spoken to, is that we will be alone, left to stew in life's sauce with no one to rouse us to a better place. And I'm not talking about the Tuesday bingo kind of better place but one that sees our worth as elders and values us. One that allows us to still be part of the greater community.

What's That on My Hand

To appreciate the gift of aging we have to let go of the idea that we are in control of our lives. I'm not saying that we have to lay down and let the wheels of life run us over. We have to bring to bear a well-centred intention – *kavanah*, as we say in the Hebrew tradition – or, to put it another way, free will, to the task of living skillfully. But we must not confuse that intentionality with control. I have always asked people to look back three years into their lives. Where were they physically, emotionally and career-wise? Could they have correctly predicted where they are right now? I have never had anyone say that they could. Why then do we insist on fixing our gaze on a future that we clearly will not have?

Permanence is the root of our bedevilment. As we age, we become aware of how little we are willing to let go: how we looked, how we worked, how we made love. Go down into the basement of your soul and see what lies there, unused and untouched. Look at all you've dragged from place to place, unexamined but firmly held.

As we journey into eldering, we send out sentries to clear the path of danger, decrepitude and disease. Every physical change, no matter how small, becomes a mortal threat – the mole that seems to appear from nowhere, the slight tremor of a finger, the yearning to rest.

Sometimes the signs are much more ominous.

It had been about a year since I had become the new me: the one with little tubes inserted in his arteries and who took four pills every day, when something happened that changed the geography of my life yet again.

I had been put on powerful blood thinners. The cardiologist who prescribed them quoted a mega-study that strongly suggested that this protocol should last a lifetime. But I was bleeding, profusely, from my nose. At the time I was still a morning jazz show host. I was alone in the studio; it was the morning shift and there was no engineer as we were a small outfit. When the warm sensation hit me anew, I would cup my hand under my nose with a handful of Kleenex I kept beside the control board. Quickly I would line up a few songs – completely contrary to station policy, and something I seemed unable to refrain from at the best of times. I would then get up and rush to the bathroom, pinching hard, hoping to form a clot that would let me finish my shift.

I went to see an ear, nose and throat (ENT) specialist. He enjoyed me on the air, he said, as he tried to look through the clots and congestion that had formed in my nose. "Can't see a thing," he said. "Don't know what's going on, but let's keep an eye on things." I left with nothing. Hoping this was nothing. "Come back in four weeks," he instructed.

Two weeks later, I woke up, looked in the mirror and to my utter shock saw that the upper part of my nose had snapped upwards. The lower part, unsupported by its cartilage, was shrunken. What on earth was going on?

Immediately I felt a dull sense of terror and sorrow. How could I reassure my wife? How could I even go out in public? I was disfigured. In one night, just one year after becoming a man with heart disease, this had happened. I can't remember how long it took to see the doctor again, but when I walked into his waiting room and sat down I was scared. He came out of his office, caught sight of me and, before he could stop himself, blurted out a loud "WHOA!" Unfortunately, the waiting room was not empty. People started to stare. Little did I realize that this was the beginning of people seeing me differently.

He composed himself and ushered me into his office. "Your septum has collapsed. I don't do this kind of work. You have to see this man," he said, giving me another doctor's information, "he's one of the best."

I did, and the new doctor, who I would grow to know well and respect, scheduled me for surgery to repair the damage . . . in five months. I figured if he thought I could wait five months then it was probably not that bad. I had switched jobs by then and was working in a crazed political environment, but this time I was not the one in the public spotlight. After years on radio and television, the persona and public face that I had constructed were gone. No longer needed.

Now if I were subject to any public gawking it was to get a

closer look at my disfigurement. One sunken nostril, a serious drop in the contour of my nose that I often masked by wearing my glasses lower than usual so as to cover the dip. By now my wife, who is sixteen years younger than me, only half-joked that she had married a lemon. I felt the sting of that but knew that I would have harboured some of the same feelings had the tables been turned. Fortunately for me, my wife is a woman of character and devotion.

The time for surgery came. Cartilage was taken from the tip of a rib and somehow placed in my nose to lift the bridge again. As I left the hospital, groggy from the general anesthetic, I saw the doctor sitting on a small ledge containing some tropical plants in the atrium off the main floor. I smiled weakly and sensed something in his return glance, something sad. But I had enough to think about with a heavily bandaged face and more than a hint of nausea from the anesthetic, so I continued on my way. My wife told me that they were sending off some of my tissue for biopsy. I tried to think nothing of it.

By then I, with the help of Dr. Google, had come up with my own diagnosis. Wegener's Syndrome, I had decided, was my problem. It could be treated with a year-long course of prednisone. Not great for the liver but not the end of the world, either.

When I returned a week later to have the bandages removed, it was obvious that the repair had only been partially successful. Where my nose met my brow was now a sizable dip. The graft had not adhered to my browbone. The nostrils were no longer wide and the nose looked thin and weak. I was, in a word, disfigured. No longer able to see myself as handsome, no longer, I would soon find out, recognizable to people who had known me for a long time. Some would walk right by; others would give my altered visage a second glance, thinking that they might know me from someplace, but then again, no.

A few days into this new reality I received a phone call while walking in a garden outside of work. It was the doctor's office; my results were in and they wanted me to come by and discuss them. Not a good sign.

My wife had a big night professionally just before the visit, something that would consume her life and her ability to be with me over the next few months. The next morning, we arrived together for the doctor's appointment. When I was called, I asked if my wife could accompany me into the room. "Of course," came the much-too-quick reply.

The doctor came in visibly stressed, with a look of pity on his face. "I'm afraid I have some very bad news for you," he said. "You have cancer."

In my forties, I'd had many friends who had been diagnosed with one form of cancer or another, and none of them had survived. I had always wondered when, not if, that word would become a part of my life.

My wife burst into tears. I did not

"What kind of cancer is it?" I asked quietly.

"It's a squamous cell carcinoma," he said.

I soldiered on: "Is it malignant?"

"Yes."

I processed this. "What's the survival rate for this?"

I was reaching the limits of what he knew – he was not an oncologist, and it was apparent that as kind and skillful a surgeon as he was, this was not his area of expertise. "I don't know for sure, but it appears to be quite high. I have booked you into Princess Margaret Hospital next Tuesday to begin tests and diagnosis for a treatment plan."

We got up to leave, and I'm not sure why but I had the presence of mind to say to him, "Thank you. I'm sorry you had to be the one to tell me." I knew that this had been hard for him. Over the next few years, we would continue to rebuild my nose to some facsimile of what it had been. We always shared a kind and respectful time together as I walked this sad and gifted path. I went home. My wife stayed downstairs while I remember going up to our bedroom and just lying on the bed as slow ripples of despair moved through me. I had always thought of death as a rude intrusion: I wasn't finished yet. What the hell are you doing this to me for? A year before I had cheated death, but now, so soon afterwards, I was not placing any bets.

My first thoughts were that I was going to let down all my children, all four of my boys. I wasn't going to fulfill my sacred obligation to be the imperfect chaperone. My older boys were in their twenties; I took some comfort in that. But my little ones were just five and two. I welled up later when I saw the littlest one. He would not even remember me, I thought. I will be someone that his mother tells the occasional story about. It was better that way. Perhaps in not cleaving to me, without us sharing the joy and disappointment that comes with being father and son, he would look kindly on me. Being gone could mean being thought of not as flesh and blood but as a soft and comforting manifestation of love.

The most powerful emotion I felt in those early days was a solid kind of sadness. It did not seem fair that I had helped to usher him into this world only to abandon him now. The first noble truth of Buddhism states that life is inherently unsatisfactory. The second says that we suffer because we live in an almost constant state of desire. My desire was to live, to not be rudely interrupted like my colleague who one day went out for a run and simply never returned. Felled by a heart attack and dead within a day. Living was not my right but my desire, and holding to this narrative was not simply a wish but my just reward.

The tests began over the next few days. I lay on an MRI table being prepped – or was it a CT scan? It all seems to be the same to me now. I looked around at the technicians behind the exam room door. These people had seen thousands of patients like me, patients who had heard those same dreaded words: *You have cancer.*

They proved to be a kind and gentle group to whom I was not simply patient #3574683. While I lay on the table, two technicians arrived with what appeared, from my limited vantage point, to be a large sheet of bone-coloured plastic mesh. "We're going to put this over your chest, neck and head. It will feel a little warm. It's to create a mask that we'll place on you later to keep your head still for some of the procedures." They applied the mesh and smoothed it over my upper body and head, gently pressing it down over the contours of my face. I lay perfectly still, feeling the cooling water trickle down my face and neck as they fashioned this strange shroud. I was a man with cancer, and this felt very much like a death mask.

I still have the mask in my garage. It's rather ghoulish looking, with two hollow eye sockets and a hole for my mouth – it looks like something out of a John Carpenter horror flick, but it's mine. I earned it and it's staying with me.

Once it had hardened enough, they removed the mask and the scans continued. If you've ever endured an MRI you know that it is a unique and, for some, terrifying experience.

I found it strangely musical. Being a fan of the ambient compositions of Brian Eno and his ilk, I lay there listening to the alternating tones and pneumatic pounding of the machine, not quite relaxing but at least intrigued. I had to lie perfectly still. I was told when to breathe and when to hold my breath. If I moved too much, they said, they would have to start all over again.

I waited two weeks for the results. I had no idea whether I would hear that the progression of my cancer was profound and my chances slim to none, or if, perhaps, a tentative thumbs-up was in the cards. My suffering soul was betting on and desiring, as the Buddha says, more time. We often bargain for more time.

Stephen Jenkinson, who believes that we are death-phobic as a society, frames the situation that many cancer sufferers find themselves in this way: *"Either you die* [. . .] *or you are killed.* There are your choices: die or be killed. Either the cancer kills you or you battle cancer and win and carry the stain of your vulnerability the rest of your shadowed days as a survivor, or the cancerous broken heart kills you and the obituary they make for you begins this way: 'After a long and courageous battle . . .'"

Though I identify with the stain of vulnerability he speaks about, I did not and do not identify as a survivor. I am not cancer. I had *a* cancer. Cancer is not a single disease – there are many kinds and many shapes. Often enough people are cured, or their remission is profound. I asked my oncologist why we never hear about the curing and healing side of cancer culture. He didn't pause before answering, "You can't raise money that way. It has to be a kill or be killed call to arms." As a communications specialist, I would say there's truth to that.

I waited. My eldest son's birthday and Father's Day passed within those two weeks. We held a party for both at my ex-wife's house. At one point she turned to my wife and said that if anything happened they could all come and stay with her. All of them. I wanted to cry. We were touched by what she said. My wife was holding us all in her arms through this, my two youngest boys and the new family we had made. Now my first marriage was also bearing such sweet fruit.

I began to see the gift inside the cancer. I know it seems odd to call what can kill you a gift, but it was. Powerful emotions ran through me. Regret, yes, some. I wished I had found a way to live in other cultures. I had long ago grown disillusioned with our high capitalist and materially obsessed western experiment. "Never got out of this town," I thought. Isn't it interesting what actually comes to mind in life's more heightened moments?

I was in a state of limbo. My identity, the personality I had worked so hard to craft over the years, had been taken by the shoulders and shaken. We construct an identity and present ourselves, or the version of ourselves we think will get us what we want in this world. Sometimes we smoke cigarettes to appear just a little reckless, dangerous, dark. Or we buy a watch or a car that says to anyone who will listen that mine is a life of quality. It doesn't really matter what props we pick to bolster our self-construction – it is and can only be a reproduction, a façade.

We always wonder what we will be able to muster when our "call" comes. Will we cower in the corner, limp with fear? Or will we become gracious and noble as we greet the angel of death? The days crawled slowly by as I waited for the results. Every time I sat to read to my little ones, I felt a surge of feeling course though me that almost burst through the dam I had constructed. I didn't want to scare them. They couldn't possibly understand that I might be leaving them soon.

The Friday before my oncologist's appointment, I was on-stage with three performers who were sharing their struggles with mental illness. I had devised a theatrical format I called Seriously Funny, where performers' serious stories could be interspersed with bursts of stand-up comedy. We would all talk for a while about the topic at hand and then I would ask if anyone had a bit about that. One would get up, and as they approached the microphone at centre stage the lights would dim and a spotlight would hit them. The comedian would do a related bit, get some laughs and then return to their chair to continue the conversation with me and the other storytellers. It was a powerful blending of sincere and entertaining moments that showcased the strength of their craft and the heartache of their journeys. That day I had two of them onstage that I had known since I was a young performer myself.

I approached one of the comedians before we got onstage, a man not known at the time for his ability to relate to others. I told him that I had been diagnosed with cancer. He clearly had no idea what to do with that information. He shrugged and muttered some sort of acknowledgement that I had said something reasonably heavy. Later he talked onstage about being a heroin addict and then diagnosed as bipolar. A few years later, he would discover that he had carried hepatitis C for years and needed a new liver. He almost died then, but in that process, you could see in his missives on Facebook that he had grown in his compassion and was humbled by the love and support that had come his way. He returned to the stage then, having had his mortality made clear, his survival worthy of deep gratitude. Unfortunately, he would eventually succumb. He was a great comic and a deeply good and wounded man.

His name was Mike MacDonald. But that day, as I told him what had happened to me, he was still in the company of those who only watched others die.

When the show was over, I left the stage and checked my cellphone. There was a message from my wife to call her right away. I did, though I didn't want to, fearful of the news. My oncologist had called while I was onstage. He told my wife that though it was malignant, the cancer had not spread to my lymphatic system. It was contained, but I would need a full course of radiation treatments.

He expected her to be relieved, but that is not her way. Eventually he said, "I'm trying to give you some good news." I chuckled a bit when she told me that part. My wife doesn't take good news very well.

We went for a more thorough consultation a few days later. The oncologist said, "This isn't what's going kill you. Something else will do that. This won't be fun, but it beats the alternative." I was, as you can imagine, relieved. He continued, "Every cancer has its own personality. Yours is a grumpy old man of a cancer. It moves nice and slow. You'll have thirty-two out of a possible thirty-five radiation sessions over a thirty-day period. You'll be here for a while every day except weekends. Your mouth will go dry, but I think we can save your salivary glands. Food will taste bad; you'll have to bulk up on protein drinks. Treatment starts in two days."

Part of me is quite practical. Though I am often the one that zooms out to thirty thousand feet when it comes to devising strategies, I can come down to earth quite quickly when the need arises. I was happy. I resolved right then that I would bring as much positive energy as I could to the radiation treatments, even though the doctor had made it clear that as the treatment progressed, I would see a steep decline in my energy and mobility.

The next day I was back to do some paperwork at what I now refer to as the Cancer Palace. Floor after floor of people who have one form or another of the diseases that make up the group of cell mutations that we call cancer. Blood cancers, bone, internal organ and my assignation, head and neck. We came to respect that we all inhabit that space in such different ways. The medicines take their toll.

One friend who years earlier I had bumped into in the X-ray department of another hospital described it well. I was there with one of my older sons because he'd separated his shoulder playing hockey, and my friend was there to take an X-ray of his foot. Turned out my friend had bone cancer. It was not a "grumpy old man of a cancer"; it was young and very aggressive. It would eventually take his life. Coincidentally, a few months later, I saw him on the same day he was told that there was nothing more that could be done. I asked him how he felt, having heard this final verdict. "Relieved, actually," he calmly said. "It's strange. First they cut you, then they burn you, then they poison you to try and kill the cancer. It's quite medieval, if you think about it. All that can stop now."

By then he had lost half his leg, yet there was something unexpectedly accepting in his voice that day. He was young enough that one might have expected more outrage. Perhaps having looked into the face of death he had found something different than you or I would expect to see. I never saw him again. I only heard of his passing. But when we met that day, he was showing me what dying with dignity might look like. It is a process, not a moment.

Now, as my own treatment progressed, I found myself sitting beside many people who were facing their mortality. Some were bargaining for one more year, month, day. Others, like me, did not want to seem too relieved that our prognosis was good. That we were still making plans and suffering gladly through our treatment.

So there I sat, day after day, waiting for my dose of radiation. The mask that had been made just for me would be placed over my head and shoulders, each clip snapped in place around the perimeter of the slab as I lay on a cold table with a U-shaped headrest as my only comfort. My body secured, the technicians would leave the room so as not to be exposed to the radiation. A small series of buzzes and clicks were my only clues that the game was afoot.

I occasionally suffer from bouts of vertigo and lying with my head straight back is one of the triggers. Halfway through my thirty-two sessions I had an attack. I began to wave my hands vigorously, something they could see on a camera mounted above me. They stopped the procedure and rushed into the room. If you've never had vertigo, I can only describe it as falling and spinning at the same time while your body is in fact doing neither.

As soon as I felt the mask release, I tried to get up off the table. They shouted at me to stop and stay still. Unbeknownst to me, the table was about seven feet in the air. That way, I realized in retrospect, the radiation gun could spin around me to shoot from many angles. I hadn't realized this in the numerous sessions I'd already gone through. They brought me down slowly and I was able to shake off the attack.

Up until that moment I had been a trooper. Now with

vertigo, repeated nosebleeds brought on by the damage done to my septum and a family busy with other important things to do, I felt utterly alone. The words of my oncologist came back to me: "This isn't what's going kill you. Something else will do that."

All around me, people were falling into two camps: those caught up in the to-and-fro of daily life and those seated beside me in the Cancer Palace still coming to terms with the finite nature of our journey and the illusory sense of control that dissolves into farce when death comes calling. I would never look at life, my life and the ever-moving river of life, in the same way again.

I have often heard tell that what people reflect on at these crucial moments is not achievement but love. Who did I love, and who did I let into my heart so that they could love me too? If that is the calculus then at what point, with what urging, do we cross the bridge into the forest of the soul? The place where we can reflect and cultivate, collecting the harvest of wisdom that has been germinating throughout our lifetimes. These are thoughts and questions that we often feel we can save for another day. But ever since that time, on that hospital table, I have been thinking about them and helping others to do the same.

Eventually the radiation and treatment regimen came to an end. I was given a bit of a peek under the hood every six months, then a once a year, and now I'm free to go about my business. I don't think I've survived, struggled with or conquered cancer. I am not a cancer survivor in the modern parlance. What I am, however, is keenly aware of my mortality and the soul-work left undone. Eventually I changed jobs. Suffice to say that aging and working brings up a whole new set of issues.

We do so little to prepare ourselves for aging, perhaps because the conversation can only lead us to something else we dread: the end, as they say. But what if you don't believe that there is an end worth pondering? That we are just a series of biological functions – electrical impulses firing off in a sequence that keeps us going, at least for a while. I have encountered many people who believe that we are quite simply born, live and die with no rhyme nor reason. That there is nothing, "No mystery to this earthly puzzle, and that to think otherwise is merely to look for some shivering comfort in the face of a meaningless void" (Frankl, *Man's Search for Meaning*).

I literally came face to face with this as I looked in the mirror, post-radiation. My nose was shrunken and malformed, my cheekbones an almost purple hue and my eyebrows bleached and mostly gone. Over the next few years I had more reconstruction work done on my nose, and eventually my normal colour returned, but I will always look different. The person I was when I stood in front of television cameras as a host of variety and current affairs programs for Canada's public broadcaster was gone.

The challenge was letting go of that "version" of myself. As we age, we all go through physical transformations. We sometimes walk by those we have known for years and realize they no longer recognize us.

I remember discussing a procedure with my ENT where he explained that he would take some cartilage from behind my ear to build up the bridge of my nose. I told him that the last two years had been a Buddhist meditation for me. Letting go of who I thought I was. Who I had been as a public persona. It was my vanity, not my nose that was rising up to demand a better fate. I'm not sure that he, as someone who also ran a cosmetic surgery business, had heard too many patients speak this way, but I do think that as a man he understood me very well.

I now run workshops on "age-ing and sage-ing," an area I was drawn to during my studies in Hashpa'ah, spiritual counselling, that build on the teachings of Rabbi Zalman Schachter-Shalomi. I once had a woman say to the group that if she was ever confined to a wheelchair that someone should put a bag over her head and shoot her. I was deeply affected by her words. I asked her why she felt that way. "Because," she said sadly, "I won't be me anymore."

I thought about her response for a moment, then responded, "Yes, you will. You'll be you in a wheelchair." We all sat with that for a moment. The conversation stayed with me for a long time afterwards.

That's Not the Way to Wash a Boy!

There are many ways to navigate the journey from child to adult and finally to elder. Many ways to identify who we think we are and what we are doing as we strap on our metaphorical tap shoes, dancing as fast as we can through this life. Mostly I have relied on the fuel of ego. I don't just mean boastfulness or bluster, though they have had their fair share of stage time. No, I mean ego in the Eckhart Tolle, Advaita Vedanta, Hindu way. The construction of a narrative that I tell myself and others is Ralph Benmergui. Not Raphael but simply anglicized, Ralph.

I bring up Tolle, *The Power of Now* bestseller, because he has written well about our lack of "is-ness" – of being present in this very moment. Like most people, I wake up every day and set about the work of adding on to the "story" of Ralph – who I have been and what will become of me, past and future. Sometimes in an easy-to-digest diet of regret and anxiety, sometimes in a much rosier scenario. But as Tolle and thousands of years of Hindu religion point out, the narrative of "I am Ralph" is not real. It's made up of foggy memories, revised scripts and fearful steps into the darkness of a future that has not yet arrived.

All this to say that what follows is part of the story of Ralph, but it is a collage and not a verifiable account. It is of my making and may not resemble who others think "Ralph" is.

I am one of four children born to Rachel (née Bengio) and Mair Benmergui. The ego has many ways of cementing our narrative in convenient places: immigrant, Jew, Sephardic Jew, Canadian, son, father, husband, comic, actor, writer, journalist, advisor, communicator. All in an effort to say, I am Ralph.

Our family of six moved to Canada in 1957. As strange as it often sounds, I was born in North Africa. At the most northwestern tip of the continent, in Tangier. A place within sight of colonialized Gibraltar and a ferry ride from Spain. I remember nothing of the city; my memories were constructed around photo albums filled with black-and-white images of another time and place. Pictures of my mother with my two older brothers, born eight and nine years before me. My sister, three years older, in a bathing suit at the beach. My mother, raven haired and buxom, holding them in her lap.

My father was one of six children, five of them boys. There were shots of him and some of his brothers looking very European as they sat together, cheering on their favourite fútbol team. There was one picture of him with a fighting cock. That's right, a rooster armed with sharp blades attached to their long legs – the better to kill their opponent with. My father looked very proud. I was culturally confused. We had eight millimetre films of bullfights, some in Spain and some in the ring in Tangier. In north Morocco, before gaining independence from France in the mid-fifties, that was allowed, though both Jewish and Muslim belief dictated that animals dying for sport was prohibited.

That independence, by the way, was the impetus for yet another moment of exile for us as Jews. I often say to people that for Jews, every country is a rental. It may be a good one for a while, maybe even a long while, but it's a rental nonetheless.

I am the youngest of our family and was only two when we left Tangier. The flight, I'm told, went from Tangier to Shetland, Scotland, then Newfoundland and finally Toronto. I was the only one who didn't vomit, so the story goes. A good start.

We moved a lot. Seven times in eight years. From right downtown to midtown in the end. I remember some things from those days, like walking with upside-down chickens swinging beside me. They were being held, two in each hand, by the man delivering them to the butcher shop up the street in Kensington Market. He would park his truck across from our walk-up apartment above a store. The cages were made of wood and the bars were thin. I think the proper term is "dowelling." The chickens squawked and my mother pulled me along, her coat smelling of damp wool. The chickens, well they were doomed, that much I knew.

Immigrating is a high-wire act for most, as it was for me. Every day you leave your family, their language, food, religion, culture and identity, and wander out into the other space. The one that has its own code and format. Your parents often have an accent and you most often don't. Their English can be shaky, and you, a child, correct them.

Their credentials no longer apply. My father had, from what I understand, done much that had meaning and some degree of status working at the Jewish hospital in Tangier, where my mother was also a nurse. It was there that they met and married.

Here in Canada my father slipped onto a lower rung of the job ladder while my mother climbed to a better place. That was hard on this gentle, frustrated man. Or so the story in my head goes. We came first, and then cousins, aunts, uncles and neighbours from back home followed. We rented a synagogue space downtown – we were making our way. The other Jews, the eastern European Ashkenazi Jews, didn't give us a second thought. All except the JIAS, Jewish Immigrant Aid Service. They sponsored us, helped us through, God love them. To give some perspective, Morocco had over a quarter of a million Jews who, for hundreds of years, lived there with relative peace, though as second-class citizens. With independence from France came waves of anti-Jewish sentiment, and today there are fewer than two thousand remaining Jews there.

It's always a rental.

Meanwhile, back in Canada, we finally drifted into a three bedroom apartment on the last street on the west side of a very well-off neighbourhood, Forest Hill. Lots of Ashkenazi Jews, lots of new money. Their lives were shaped by the intergenerational trauma of the Holocaust. We Moroccans had not experienced that murderous horror first-hand, but to this day I am haunted by it. I cry, I shake inside and wonder not how God could have let this happen but how humanity could have let this happen.

By now I was in grade three and getting very embarrassed. Every time we moved, I would have to hear some new teacher mangle both my names: Rafee-il Benmengooey. Sheepishly I would raise my hand on day one, shirt done to the collar and pants hiked up, Urkel style. "Here . . ." I vowed to eradicate this shaming ritual as soon as I could. I noticed that there was a teacher in the school named Miss Ralph. Scottish, I believe. Now, in my head, I add a few layers to this part of the story – always have. I had noticed that in TV credits – TV being my portal to how to be like the white Christian nation we were surrounded by – there would occasionally be some producer or writer named Ralph. Miss Ralph, TV Ralphs. Sold. I remember getting a quiz sheet and perhaps for the first time writing "Ralph Benmergui" at the top. Nobody had made me sell out. There was no Ellis Island customs clerk draining the ethnicity out of me, changing Schwartz to Smith. No, I was the author of my own demise, and I regret it to this day. Once I became a public figure it seemed impossible to turn back, and it still does. I am in a cage of my own design.

Years passed. I taught myself to skate, slithering around on my ankles till I was twelve. I played hockey in house leagues, even made the all-star team that my friends were on. Me, a hockey player, made the school team, too. My parents never came to see me. The space between their world and what was now mine grew larger.

They did, however, see me get on a stage and perform. From the beginning, I have always been very comfortable on a stage and conversely uncomfortable as an audience member. Perhaps it is my tendency to be a know-it-all or my competitive nature that gave me a little voice in my head that often says, "What are they doing up there, give me that mic. You gotta be more like this." Forgive me for letting that little voice out but it is best, I find, to welcome all the parts of who you are into the conversation.

I remember being in a play at the local synagogue every year. This particular year someone already in the business, as it were, had written a parody of *Fiddler on the Roof* entitled *Gong on the Roof*. A show that clearly wouldn't be kosher in this age, and that's all the better. Nonetheless, at the time it was "acceptable." Just before the night of our performance in front of four hundred people, I had to go to the dentist. A trip I have made way too many times in my life. He froze my mouth, and I kept asking for more freezing out of a well-founded terror of pain. By the time I got backstage I had lost all feeling in half of my face. I remember peeking through the curtains to see if my dad was out there. He'd said he'd come. I scanned as best I could, and just when I had surrendered to the idea that he was once more a no-show, I gave one more cursory glance to the front row and – there he was in his resplendent swarthiness amid all these "other" Jews sitting, fidgeting with the thin paper program. Oh my God, not only had he shown up he was going to be looking right up my nostrils. I don't remember much else about that night except when the writer-director, a wonderful man named Alan Gordon, gave us notes at intermission. "Yes, and Ralph, you're doing great, but could you please stop looking at the audience after every joke?" Good note.

One thing I should add that coloured everything about my childhood – well, actually, two things. First, I was the kind of kid who had to look through the husky rack when my mother would take me to buy my once-every-two-years' suit. Chunky, you could say. When they were splitting up boys in gym class for team sports, they would make half of us shirts and half of us skins. I was mortified. No good would come from me being relegated to the skins team. I didn't care who had a better team, all I cared about was who had a better stomach. Kids are cruel. "Hey, fatso, nice boobs," they'd say. Throughout school, all the way till university, I was the kind of boy that girls really liked to talk to about other boys – boys that they really liked. Like a lot of heavier kids, I called the comedian in me out to keep everybody laughing. Keep everybody wanting me around, even if it was just to yuk it up. I was good at it, too. I could make almost anybody laugh, kid or adult. I had this ability to read the room.

Every Sunday I stayed glued to the TV (black and white) watching *The Wonderful World of Disney*, *Bonanza* and the unbelievable, culture-shifting career launcher that was *The Ed Sullivan Show*. Years later I would tell a network executive that I wanted to do what Ed did – stand onstage in a suit (a tuxedo actually) and introduce an all-Canadian Sullivan-esque show once a week to celebrate Canadians.

Jackie Mason flippin' the bird at Ed and killing his career for a few decades, Alan King doing mother-in-law jokes, Stiller and Meara, and the Canadian comedy duo that made more appearances than any other act, Wayne and Shuster. I adored them. I wanted to be them. In grade four, Mr. Parhboo let us put on a show every Friday in a class he called Topics of Interest. A friend and I performed Wayne and Shuster sketches verbatim. It was great. Mr. Parhboo, by the way, also made me stand at the back of the class for the entire day once for forgetting, or not doing, an assignment. The result was that I became quite nauseous and deposited the contents of my lunch on the back of Susan – easily the most beautiful girl in class. Bad moment, but great fodder for future retellings in my efforts to get kids to pay attention to Ralphie.

The second part adds a dark piece to my self-portrait: I was a bedwetter. For a long time, too. Actually, until the night before my bar mitzvah and never again. Sounds a bit like a Mordecai

Richler character, but no, it was actually me. No sleepovers (unless we were related), no overnight camp and way too many interrupted sleeps for my poor mother. I later found out my brothers had suffered the same affliction – something I would have appreciated knowing considering how many times they taunted me about it.

It's hard keeping secrets about yourself. It's hard feeling lesser-than. In the end, once I was through the gauntlet of childhood, the world opened up to me just a little.

Three things happened: I finally got a girlfriend, I got really good at being funny and I became very sad. My last high school yearbook entry said, simply, "I'm sick of being the class clown. You run out of jokes after a while."

The next year would change many things for me, including how I saw my life. I enrolled at a local university, the one everybody with a less than 90 percent average could take refuge in.

On my first day of classes, as I wandered around the large array of faceless, Stalin-esque buildings, I stumbled upon a strange sight – a chalk outline of a body. Later I found out that a graduate student had jumped off the building above and ended his, or her, life. Just like that. On the first day of school.

I hated being at that school. Lecture halls with hundreds of mostly bored students. In most cases, the professor, a sage on the stage, would appear equally bored. I started skipping classes. No one noticed – this wasn't high school. If you wanted to drift off that was your choice. But what was I supposed to be doing here? I had always had great difficulty in school. At the time no one thought to call it ADHD. You were just a disruptor, unable to pay attention to the details, surviving while those around you thrived.

I was getting more and more depressed as I realized that

I had not been living an authentic life. My girlfriend's mother was a kind and loving woman. Groomed to be a good suburban housewife, she was anything but. She seemed to see who I was even if I didn't. She encouraged me to read the emerging psychotherapeutic writings of pioneers like Fritz Perls, father of Gestalt; Arthur Janov, of Primal Therapy fame; Carl Rogers, with his landmark book, *On Becoming*. Books on schooling, like *Summerhill* by A.S. Neill and John Holt's *What Do I Do Monday?* My mind was exploding. But at the same time, my girlfriend had lost interest in me, I was adrift at school and I withdrew.

I stopped socializing, stayed in my room at my parents' new apartment and suffered the first bout of what would become a series of anxiety attacks that would possess me for a few painful months at a time through my early twenties. The pain in my chest was crushing. My doctor's advice was simply to take it easy. Thanks, Doc. I ate less and less. My mother would beg me to come out of my room and at least eat a boiled egg, anything. Over a period of several months I dropped about forty pounds. My body was trim, my facial features chiselled. When I looked in the mirror of the medicine chest, where I had found a stash of Valium that I would take once a day, I saw someone I didn't know I could be. All this pain and sadness had birthed a new me. For the first time in my life, I was handsome.

This was a terrible and dangerous way to change, but I did not plan for it to happen.

I remember going to school during this time and occasionally finding that girls I had known my whole life had started doing double takes and acting more appreciative to the formerly chubby, loud and obnoxious Ralph they had grown up with. I didn't like it. I was mad. "Oh, I get it, now I'm worth saying hello to." I thought this though I never said it. It was my first lesson in impermanence. I was now a fat kid in a romantic lead's body. Anxiety attacks and all.

Through that first change, my loyal best friend, and to this day one of my true guardian angels, stuck by whatever version of Ralph I served up. He was Mike. He died when we were forty-three. Though we drifted apart after that first year of university, we came back together before he passed. I miss him. I love him. The angel of my second change was and is the love of my life, my wife. If the price of love is grief then mine, in light of her loving kindness for me, will be immeasurable.

It is no great tribute to my first post-secondary school experience that I indeed passed the year. And then I left. Everything. I auditioned for theatre school at what was one of the best schools for drama studies in Canada, the University of Alberta. Sixteen students were cherry-picked from around the country, though I didn't make the cut my first time around. I found that out on the day I got fired from a job that my friend had found for me at his dad's warehouse. I deserved to get fired – I was mouthy, a verbal kind of bully, and one day, for the second time in my life, the object of my undeserved scorn turned around and punched me in the face. The blow landed on my chin and sent me stumbling back. All the great reading I had been doing on becoming a better me, all the pain I had suffered from anxiety, none of that mattered at that moment. Later that week I was fired.

I came home to a letter from the drama school saying that I had not been accepted but that I had been shortlisted for possible entry. A few weeks later, I was in. My parents didn't have a lot of money. I was their last of four and now I wanted them to send me away – not to law school or to become a dentist, or some other career that would actually pay. No, I was off to be an . . . actor.

I remember telling my father that I wanted to be an actor. I'm sure he had more than an inkling, having sat in the front row and watched me ham it up in front of four hundred strangers. Still, this was not something I looked forward to sharing with him. "Dad, I want to go away to school to become an actor." Now here is a moment where I can tell you I distinctly remember how my father reacted to the news. Where I concretized a moment from forty-five years ago so that the facts bend to my narrative. But this is why memories are more a collage of self-sustaining myths that we use to bolster our stories. All I can say is that I have assigned my father the part of the disappointed immigrant dad who hoped I wouldn't have squandered all that he had given up to make for us a new life in the play called *Ralph*. Truth is, I have no idea what he thought that day.

Telling my mother, on the other hand, is much clearer in my mind. We were standing in our narrow little kitchen when I told her. "Well, it's about time," she said.

It was a liberating moment.

Ralph Becomes Raphael

For the second time in my life, at the age of nineteen, I was getting on an airplane. This time I wasn't with my family travelling from centuries of North African and Andalusian life to Canada. This time I was travelling from the centre of my Canadian universe to the roughneck petro state of Alberta.

I wasn't alone. One of my high school friends was also coming to attend the Fine Arts program at the University of Alberta. A Jewish family that his parents knew put us up for a few days until we found a place to rent on the south side of Edmonton. The North Saskatchewan River cuts through the centre of Edmonton, with several bridges spanning its shores. We found a house and soon a couple of roommates to help shoulder the rent. For the first time in my life I was truly away from home.

I was exhilarated. For nineteen years I had constructed battlements around my sense of who I was. Mostly it was rearguard action that I used to try and hide myself from others. I had been chubby, called Dumbo by some family members, carried the shame of being a bedwetter like a heavy sack and, as I tried to say when leaving high school, a worn-out class clown. So now, with only one person knowing who I "was," perhaps I could start anew. Make a different Ralph, an actor who didn't need to be funny to stay in the conversation.

I began to explore the city. Crossing over onto the north side I came face to face with a reality that back east was confined to one street corner deep in the downtown. The shameful truth of the decimation of our original peoples – the cultural genocide of the Indigenous population in Canada. As I milled about 97th Street, I stared at passed-out Indigenous men in tree pots outside an upscale hotel; at men and women sitting on the curb, brown paper bag in hand, so drunk that they didn't even register that I was slowly walking by. Not even a glance. In later years, when living in Winnipeg, the tragedy of our country's abuse and neglect found an even deeper well in my soul. We as Canadians often speak of human rights in other countries – we would in the years to come boycott South Africa, tsk tsk at the racialized oppression in the United States, and damn the Soviets and Chinese for their draconian regimes. But here, in the ancestral lands of so many First Nations, we have trampled their treaty rights, shuttled them off to government-subsidized ghettos, robbed them of their languages and cultural rights, and literally stolen their children. At that moment in Edmonton, I had come face to face with people dead on their feet. Lost in a maze of bricks, glass and steel. It made, and still makes, me wonder just who in the hell we think we are.

The West was an entirely different ecosystem than the one

I grew up in. The sky is so big that you swear you could reach out and touch it. Clouds stretch forever to the horizon, and in Edmonton they say that the smoke from heavy industry adds a burst of colour to each night's sunset. I was shown around by one of our hosts, taken to the university campus. In the parking lot I saw posts with electrical plugs stuck in the asphalt every two spaces. "What's all that about?" I asked. My host looked at me, puzzled. "Are you serious?" he said. "Yeah what's it for?" He smiled. "It's to plug in your car." I was at a loss.

My host laughed. "You really aren't from here." Then he explained: "You see, it gets so cold that you have to have a block heater under the hood that makes sure that the gas line doesn't freeze, among other things. At a party in a prairie winter you have to occasionally get your parka back on and go outside to start your car if no plug is around. Otherwise you have to leave your frozen car behind."

Wow! I thought. Tough town.

So, you wanna be in showbiz?

It was day one of acting school and I was terrified. This was supposed to be one of the top three schools in the country. Sixteen kids, that's it, with only five or six expected to make it through to fourth year. As everybody sat in a circle and introduced themselves to the group, my fellow thespians spoke of being in this major production or that film. Just about everybody had been in Thornton Wilder's *Our Town*. Everybody except me. The groups were also completely white and Christian. This was 1975. The oil boom was in full swing – a period of time that politicians forty years later would lament the passing of. That day, in that room, the privilege and exclusivity of my cohort were just a matter of fact.

They were probably wondering how I got in. Hell, everybody but me had been in *Our Town*, and I didn't even know that it was a play. Then it was my turn to introduce myself. "Hi, my name is Ralph, actually it's Raphael," I began. Immediately the professor, a round man with a deep, butter-smooth voice stopped me. "Oh," he cooed. "Raphael, that's much better, we will call you Raphael." Red flag number one. You see, in proclaiming naming rights he had already managed to pronounce my name as Rafeeal. That's not how you say it. That's what I should have said, but he was the sage on the stage, literally. Who was I to point out that the very reason I had stopped using it was because it was apparently too ethnic to pronounce properly.

I was now Raphael again, with some minor mangling. Acting school was intense and a highly personal experience. We had ballet three times a week. I had to wear tights, though I passed on the rather snug dance belt. Chubby boy was still adjusting to this newfound svelte body. If only my classmates knew that I had never taken a dance class in my life, and that the klutz flitting by was actually a fake, an impostor, they would have understood that all these chaînés turns were making me very dizzy. Actually, I'm sure that watching me career into the change area beside the floor-to-ceiling mirrors might have been clue enough.

While others flew around the dance studio, whipped along by the southern drawl of our taskmaster, I counted the minutes till the class would end. That dance teacher was quite the character. He was also interested in me in a sexual way, but I wasn't game. I've always thought that rejection had a real effect on my fortunes as the year progressed.

There is a belief in many acting circles that you must break down the actor – strip the person down to an emotional skeleton and then rebuild them with a much deeper understanding that they have within them all the characters they will ever play. One of our better teachers taught me that. You are indeed capable of being anything in this life – a saint, a cheat, a lover and, yes, even a murderer. It's all a matter of circumstance and choices. Actors that are truly inspired make remarkable choices.

Later on in my short-lived acting career, I saw all that in my friend Maury Chaykin. Maury played the deranged cavalry commander manning a godforsaken outpost that Kevin Costner journeys to in the movie *Dances with Wolves*. Maury had an uncanny ability to look at a script, put it down and inhabit the character in a way that others could never hope to realize.

Most of the actors and artists I know are secular in their spirituality. They don't see religion as being compatible with freedom. As for me, I wish I could have joined my spiritual/religious side with my need-to-be-loved performer side while still in those funny dance tights. The personality tear-down that I now realized was not in the brochure but which was essential to the mission of the teaching staff became, in the wrong hands and at certain times, toxic.

This toxicity, as is the case with other arts schools, extended to after-class activities as well, where the house party was truly a thing. We would gather at someone's home near the university – I have no idea whose house it was back then, but the parties were intense. Actors didn't just dance to the music; they moved as if their lives depended on it. Kitchen conversations weren't small talk. No, they were big, very big talk. The professors would be there, too, making it so that we weren't just hanging out; we were, in a sense, auditioning.

One of those professors was also the head of the department and our acting teacher. He sat across the room from me at one soiree. He caught my eye and beckoned me toward him. I don't remember much else, but I do remember that he pointed at me, and in the tradition of a Roman emperor he slowly turned his thumb downward and muttered, "You could be something, but you're not, you're . . ."

I don't recall exactly what he said next. Memory, it's a trickster. Was I a nobody, a fake, a failure? It hardly matters. After a lifelong quest for spiritual healing I have arrived at a place where being present makes memory and past just that: past. Not irrelevant but more of a watercolour painting, softened images and blurred landscapes of moments to which we continually add colour and shading.

Years later, when I was co-hosting a national current affairs TV show, that very same Caesar was a guest star on the popular Canadian TV show *Street Legal*. They were taping in the next studio. Some of the actors were my friends. I didn't know he would be there and as I walked onto the set to say hi I saw him. By then a dozen years had passed.

"Rapheeal!" he said as he approached. "Good to see you." We spoke for a moment and then he paused. "Did we make a mistake by letting you go back then?" he asked, in a gentle tone. I could have said, "Damn right you did, and look at me now. Hell, look at you!" But I would be dishonest if I said that had come to mind.

It's funny, that moment we have later in the day after someone has hurt or scared you; the moment where as a kid you stood in front of the bathroom mirror and, with a bit of gunslinger in your voice, said everything you couldn't think to say in the moment. But in that instant what came out of me was something that, in retrospect, was akin to a moment of grace. "No, you didn't make a mistake. It all worked out for the best." His smile was one of relief.

We are not responsible for what others do or say, only what actions we ourselves take. Each night before bed, observant Jews recite what's called the "bedtime Shema." It's powerful. A time for humility. A challenging statement of compassion uttered before we drift off to the dream world, the land of souls. "I forgive those that have hurt me today, whether unintentionally or intentionally." Think about that. Someone knowingly hurt you and your reaction is to absolve them.

If I had turned instead to my old teacher and pointed, slowly turning my thumb down, I would not have felt better at that moment. I would have been filled with hurt and anguish. I would be drinking the poison of revenge in hopes of killing the other man.

To live is to be wounded – it is how we tend to the wounds we suffer and inflict that mark the quality of our journey.

By now you know that I was eventually kicked out of drama school and left Edmonton behind. Lots happened there. I was seduced by a powerful woman and then terrified as a jealous and fearsome man, who I didn't know was in the picture, came looking for me. He seemed to be in every room I entered. I was convinced he was going to inflict something much more serious than a scornful thumbs-down on very naive, young me. In the end, he settled for shooting me deeply alarming glances. It was time to head back to Toronto.

The next few years were a gift I will never forget. I was in honest-to-God showbiz. Acting, writing, even directing. I was in the show voted the worst play of 1979. I wore a gold lamé jockstrap in a parody called *Reefer Gladness*. We used to peer out behind the curtain to count how many misguided patrons had ponied up a few dollars. The rule, which I'm pretty sure we made up, was if there were more of us backstage than out in the audience we didn't have to go on.

Out of nowhere I talked my way into a job as an overnight social worker at a house residence for emotionally disturbed teenagers. Two things I learned there: one, that I could talk my way in and out of almost anything; and, much more importantly, that mental illness and the destruction it wreaks on families is deeply and profoundly heartbreaking for all involved. We break an arm and everyone frets over us; we suffer mental illness, and we are left shunned and alone. Very much alone. To those that don't give up, that reach toward others and not away from, it is a task that reaps little obvious reward. But God love you for your work.

While working overnight at the home, I was also doing something else: writing my very first stand-up act. It all started because I happened to know the men behind the birth of what would turn out to be the home of stand-up comedy in Canada, Yuk Yuk's Comedy Cabaret. Mark Breslin and Joel Axler had both been just ahead of me at Forest Hill Collegiate in midtown Toronto. Mark had been a bit of a Sith Lord at my high school. Small in physical stature, he had been put upon by his classmates, but he eventually found a way to take his revenge on the entire school. He launched a phantom candidate to run for school president and convinced the majority of the student body to vote for him. He was already on the road to being the sort of disrupter that would one day build a national chain of comedy clubs.

But right then, in 1976, Mark had established a space in the iconic 519 Church venue, in the heart of the emerging gay village. He called the club Yuk Yuk's, and for a buck you could climb down the stairs to the bowling lane–sized basement and take a seat. Comics would be introduced, they'd walk up the middle between two rows of customers and in five minutes those comics tried to do something very hard to pull off: make the audience laugh.

Stand-up is brutal. Consider the language of it: you kill, you die, you bomb. People come demanding that you make them do something violent. Laugh out loud. Not snicker. Not smile, but from their belly explode into laughter. You just can't fake it.

When we watch a stage drama, half the time we feel inadequate if we dislike it. "It must be me, after all this is art I'm seeing."

But in stand-up you are either funny or you're dead. I had made another decision: I was going to put myself onstage and subject myself to the lion's den of comedy.

I went down to Yuk Yuk's and hung out as soon as the club opened. I watched a parade of would-be comics get up and do their thing. Some were good and some weren't. In the parlance of the genre, many were dying up there. To this day watching a comic bomb is truly heartbreaking for me. You get up there. You're on your own with no one to lean on, no one to blame. You throw out a joke you've written, practised and banked on. And they just sit there, staring. Fight, flight or freeze. Usually it's flight. You speed up, pumped full of fearful adrenalin. As time goes on you become more confident. They don't laugh and you actually slow down as if to say, "Fuck you, I'm funny." Works a charm. But that night I was just watching. Still safe in my own judgments.

I came away that night thinking that I was at least as funny as these guys – and they were almost always guys at first. On the way out I asked Mark if I could get on. Mark said, "Fine, two weeks from now, you get five minutes. Show up a few minutes early and I'll tell you what number you are in the lineup."

It was now time to be funny on demand, just like on the playground at school. Please welcome fat boy Ralph back to the stage after a valiant post-secondary escape attempt. After all, that version of me had helped me survive the *Lord of the Flies*–esque smackdown of many a recess. It seems to me that we live and die many times in our short lives. One version of me is born, and I furiously renovate that persona until it starts to show cracks and then crumbles at various speeds into dust, and then that Ralph/Raphael dies. In this case, I reached back to put on the clown outfit.

I showed up two weeks later for my next shot. The comics were herded into the back of the basement in a boiler room. A few were smoking a joint. Though I was a regular pot smoker, I knew that, for me, performing and pot did not go together. I needed to be able to feel the audience, to be present and to connect with the unpredictable beast that on any given night might forge a mystical consensus. One crowd could be hyper and receptive, another grumpy and expectant. No one had taken a vote; they just melded minds. And my job, our job as performers, was to reach them, speak some semblance of common experience and truth, and make them love us. Make them love me. What a strange thing to do.

My name was called. I sauntered up the aisle with a cigarette in hand and sat on the edge of the stool – the only thing that adorned the otherwise bare stage. Behind me was a brick wall with a Yuk Yuk's sign affixed to it. I could barely see through the adrenalin that coursed through my body. The amble up the aisle had been all show. Now I had to rein in my energy and remember what I had practised leading up to this, in front of a mirror in the attic of a residence for emotionally disturbed teenagers. My first bit, one that I had practised for a week, was not some piece of Lenny Bruce–inspired wit and irony. No, my first bit was about *The Flintstones*. "Didya ever notice that Wilma has no eyes? She has dots, black dots. If she had eyes, maybe she'd notice that Fred's been wearing the same fucking suit for seventeen years." They laughed – not hard, but they laughed a little as I babbled on for my five minutes. It was enough for Mark to let me come back. There were some really good, polished comics that night. One was a local FM deejay. He had a twelve-string guitar, played it left-handed if I remember correctly. His presence onstage was electric. His name was Rick Moranis. He would go on to star on *SCTV* and in film, and then turn his back on the whole damn thing years later, staying home to raise his kids. I love him for that.

Eventually, not too far down the line, we – and I say we, because stand-up is a clan that borders on being a cult; once in, you're in it for life – moved into a real, honest-to-God nightclub. Yuk Yuk's had arrived. We found ourselves on the eastern flank of the burgeoning Yorkville scene. The neighbourhood had transitioned from a hippie enclave filled with head shops, eclectic bookstores and unisex hair salons to the disco, high-end boutique epicentre of the late seventies, early eighties cocaine-and-powder-blue-jumpsuits crowd. We definitely didn't belong. We were a bunch of loud-mouthed, mostly socially crippled truth tellers, *Flintstones* notwithstanding.

With drama school in the rear-view mirror, I was living the Ed Sullivan dream – comic, singer in a local cover band doing sixties tunes. I had to do it. I knew that I would never get the chance again. It wasn't a life path, more just a crazy, fun ride.

The club was a hit and some of the gang were already separating themselves from the herd, soon to become some of the best anywhere. Mike MacDonald, Norm Macdonald (no relation but both from Ottawa), and the biggest acts, Howie Mandel and Jim Carrey. The second tier would go on to become great writers, showrunners and journeymen comics, and would carve out a living for decades to come. Then there were the unappreciated ones. Savants like Steve Shuster, son of my boyhood idol Frank Shuster of Wayne and Shuster fame. People would introduce him as Wayne and Shuster's son, as if the duo had conceived him. It was a heady time. Steve and I cooked up a musical parody medley as the cheesy Vegas lounge act Sandler and Young. I was the smouldering Latino Sandler, with an open shirt and big collar; Steve was the avuncular if not dim-witted Ralph Young. We had a blast. Comics were, and are, fiercely competitive, yet we fused together effortlessly, charged with so much creativity, fear and elation.

Every night we watched the crowd file out, locked the doors and took turns jumping up on the stage, praying that something totally fucking brilliant would come out of our mouths. Something that would receive the blessing of another comic who would turn to us and say, "That's funny," delivering the news in a deadpan, oncologist-in-a-consultation kind of way.

Every night we walked into the fire. Some of us got burned while others, like true firewalkers, didn't even get singed. The first to leave the Yuk Yuk's stratosphere and go into showbiz orbit was Howie Mandel. He could walk off the stage and rightly declare, "I super-killed!" Everyone was buzzing about Howie. No one wanted to follow him. There were two kinds of comics back then: those who wanted to hear the roar of the crowd, whatever the cost; and those that wanted to become comedy warriors, ready to share the gospel of truth to power. Howie fell within the first category. He was, and I mean this as a compliment, a clown. A true clown with impeccable timing and the ability to say almost nothing and yet have the audience clutching their sides in fits of laughter. I mean, he got up on that stage in nothing but a diaper and spit out baby talk gibberish and they went wild. For those of us with a bit more of the preacher in us, it was depressing.

Then there was the punk-infused, raw and dangerous energy of the late, great Mike MacDonald. Mike took no prisoners, got along with almost no one and unfortunately taught me that you can be great at what you do, but if you piss off enough people you won't be getting that call to showbiz fame. At least not in little old Canada – the pool here just wasn't big enough for you to poop in. This is another one of Howie's bits by the way.

Mike's tennis racket "air guitar up in the attic" piece was pure rock and roll genius, and yes, it super-killed! Mike and I always got along. He had decided that he liked me, that I might be going places, too. We just didn't know at the time that we were headed in different directions.

Then there was Jim Carrey. Most know his backstory by now, but what always intrigued me about him was his courage.

Whenever something looked like his ticket to fame, he would throw it over his shoulder and reinvent. Jim has always had a place in my heart. I have only seen him once or twice since he became an American star. His talent and elasticity put him in a league of his own, but beyond that I always rooted, and still do hope, for him to be a happy person.

Stand-up was a time of limitless exhilaration, deep doubt and a sense of true belonging. I lived in many worlds at once: Actor, sort of. Singer, oh what the hell, sure. And the most exclusive club of all, stand-up comedian. Even the Second City types would ask: How on earth do you do it? I would never have the guts for that. We were tightrope walkers in the Yuk Yuk's circus. No pay, tons of laughs and a healthy dollop of sexual energy flowing through our veins. We roamed the back hall throwing bits at each other, waiting for that golden reply – a "that's funny," or simply shaking our heads and saying, "Seventeen, that's funnier than eleven."

Mark Breslin, our ringleader and provocateur, would dare the comfy crowd to laugh. Steal a purse, bring it onstage and tear apart its owner. Backstage we'd wait like restless hyenas. Through the narrow passageway to the tiny stage in the blackened nightclub, we would be called. There truly is nothing like walking onto that stage – the rush of adrenalin blasting through your body on a Saturday night, the room packed, all eyes on you. Are you going to kill or die?

Up there you are alone. I would stare into the black middle space of the crowd and speak to the group psyche. They wanted truth – your truth, their truth – but wrapped in laughter and, if you were really good, some tears as the crowd roiled and surged through the night. Then there was the other side. The joke that had killed for five shows in a row that just comes out of your mouth and lands in front of you onstage like a comedy hairball, dead on arrival. The audience sits there, disappointed. You have two choices then: look them in the eyes and stare right back like some gunslinger at high noon, or back down. What's at stake is who gets to decide what's funny. If you want to come back the next night, you better lean in.

Jim, Howie, Simon Rakoff, Lawrence Morgenstern, Lou Dinos. The Nip n Tuck Tubbrag, Chas Lawther and Suzette Couture. There were so many comrades-in-arms. We learned, we stole, we even grabbed a sandwich from a waitress's plate in the kitchen in lieu of pay. If presence and contemplation are the gifts of age, then this was the absolute opposite – all guts and glory. Our egos dragging us onstage every night that we could get a spot. We heckled each other or barked an editorial laugh of approval from the back of the club on a mostly empty Tuesday night.

Some of us became less themselves, lost in their stage personas. Carrey was and is a great impersonator, and that was just the first rung on the ladder to fame – he was just getting warmed up. Howie Mandel could magically stand on a stage and just keep repeating the word "okay-okay . . . okay . . . okay, okay, okay." Worked every time.

Me, well I was doing characters onstage back then. Some were good, like my Jewish American Princess, Shelly; others were more actor-ish, like the monologue where I played a gay bar-hopper and a biker switching from one to the other mid-sentence. In the end they go home together. Whenever I would finish this bit there would be some guy in the front staring up at me uncomfortably. I took that as a red cape. I'd ask if they thought I was gay and then growl, "If I were, what makes you think I'd want to sleep with you?"

I was getting attention, and like any young and craven performer I sucked at handling it. I am by nature introverted – my onstage bluster was all a cover. In fact, most comics are, at best, awkward. As someone who came from acting, most of them saw me as a dilettante and way more normal than the rest of the herd. Most if not all had great rhythm – many of us played the drums to some degree. You have to have a great sense of rhythm to refine the craft of joke-telling. It's called . . . timing.

I slowly moved away from my characters – they were a dead end. I started hosting. It was the practical side of me that led me to it. If you had an act, you could only play a gig outside the club twice, maybe three times in a year. But if you hosted, you could return every few weeks. What I loved about it was how every night was different. You had to be right there, with the audience, and ride it like a bucking bronco. But you had three, four, maybe even five chances to build that momentum through the evening as you introduced act after act.

I liked the tension of stand-up. The raw nerves of hitting a societal funny bone. But in the end, I had a choice: become a character that I could play every night, one that got a ton of laughs, or begin a journey to become myself – a journey that continues to this day.

On a spiritual level I was lost. Yearning for approval, trying to get whatever I could but hoping that no one noticed while I scurried about in the shadows. The nagging feeling that had followed through my young life, the thought that I wasn't myself, was back. I felt I was only a collection of reactions. The reaction to being an immigrant, to being fat, to being the wrong kind of Jew, to becoming handsome out of nowhere. The paradox was that I was no longer fat, I was acceptable. Hell, I could be famous. I was a steaming mess of contradictions. I had an inner life that had been forged in the sadness and shame of past experience, an emerging yearning for true self, and no life map to get there.

I went to a place that no one from my upbringing had gone to. I went to a therapist to take a chance and begin a new journey. Primal Therapy was big then. It had been invented by Arthur Janov in the States and was designed to unleash the raw pain that we carry so deeply.

These days there are well-researched approaches that emphasize how the body keeps score. Back then there was little support for doing this kind of work. I cried, I wailed, I hugged the pillow of my sorrow. Though I didn't pursue that therapy for long, it did make me realize that I was in a great deal of pain. That I had been gaslit when it came to expressing such feelings in my family environment. But despite that, the best approach for me was to bring that sad/angry boy into the light.

By now, the eighties had arrived, I was occasionally taking hallucinogenic drugs – LSD and magic mushrooms. For years, the messaging was that we would all become lost if we took these substances. That we would microwave our cats. Luckily, I didn't have either a microwave or a cat. We were also warned that we would go insane. That proved a little more possible. One of the best comedians of our generation did experience mental illness while on a psilocybin trip we shared, and he was never the same again.

For me, however, the trips were inspiring. A sort of shortcut to the gates of spiritual awakening. No, the feeling didn't last, but I caught a glimpse of the "Doors of Perception," as Huxley called them. I sat on the flat second-floor roof at a party one night and looked up into the night sky. It all seemed so perfectly, laughably clear. The cosmic joke came into focus – we are molecular in the body of creation. Think about us, sitting on a dirtball planet in a minor solar system, in a swirl of hundreds of millions of galaxies. One winter night I sat on a porch, tripping on LSD and keeping company with a neighbourhood cat. His profoundly simple presence was revelatory for me. There was no yesterday for that cat, no tomorrow to fear or crave. Just this moment, on this porch. In the garden in front of us stood a tree surrounded by snow. But wait, there was no snow tucked up tight around its trunk. That space had thawed. The tree was generating heat. Living.

There is a great meditative prayer in Jewish Renewal liturgy:

> As we breathe out what the trees breathe in,
> And the trees breathe out what we breathe in,
> So we breathe each other into life,
> We and You.

For many who take the hallucinogenic journey there comes with it a profound understanding of the interconnectedness of all that is. We are the drop and we are the ocean. Imagine being twentysomething and having the universe unlock a secret for you that could change you forever. Imagine.

But still the anxiety remained. The ego came charging to the rescue. The attention seeking pushed me onto stand-up stages, theatre openings and into rickety rock band vans as I wrapped myself in a shroud of dope smoking, wearing my sunglasses as we drove down highways from one lousy gig to the next.

Until I started to yearn for actual love. I hadn't had many real relationships. One, to be exact, and that just dribbled away when she found herself longing for someone else. I didn't even know it had happened. Now I was just a roaming young man. It's quite something, that juvenile chapter of love. Trying to mimic the often-bad examples we grew up with, and trying not to, as well. Trying out the jealous guy, the sensitive guy, the count-on-me guy. I sucked at all of them.

Yuk Yuk's was where I and many of my comedy colleagues actually found our mates: one with the restaurant manager, another with the box-office girl and me with a waitress. The other two married them and stayed that way for keeps. I, on the other hand, had twenty years and two boys with mine, and to this day we are still friends. Little did I know that the biggest job in life would be fathering. It still is. I ended up with four boys in two cohorts, twenty years apart.

Singing in a little rock band, telling jokes, occasionally being on some cheesy TV show. Even acted in a few movies – Canadian movies of the early eighties, mind you.

Sounds great, right? Then why did I feel so lonely, so terribly anxious. Anxiety attacks, three in five years, were the wake-up call of my early twenties. Friends tolerated my boorishness, family faded into the background. I was a young man on the run from myself.

My body was telling me that I couldn't go on this way. Something had to give. But I had already told everyone I knew that I was an actor, a comedian, a somebody. I had walked home for lunch in elementary school practising my Oscar speech. When Timothy Hutton, who was roughly my age, won the award for best actor – or was it supporting actor? – for his role in *Ordinary People*, I watched and I cried tears of envy but also fear. Fear that I would never achieve my very big dreams. I watched in awe when Mort Sahl, the legendary truth-telling comedian, hit the stage at Yuk Yuk's. He could be dead serious about the things that really mattered – politics, race riots, the death of the American dream – and then save the audience from annihilation by telling a good old-fashioned joke. Again, I watched and I cried. I would never be that true, that good, that authentic.

I was on the wrong path. The pain in my chest was telling me so. The tears were proof that I had to reimagine myself. I had to quit this acting thing, I told my theatre friends. "What?! But that's what you are," they said. I watched as some climbed the pole of showbiz success and others just kept slipping back down again. Over the years I have found those that have had a fall from grace to be more interesting. It's not a morbid, car-crash interest. There is a choice we must make when we fall from a great height. We can wallow in resentment and jump back into the fray, seeking revenge, or we can look inside and take the spiritual opportunity that a broken heart presents. The public life, as I was discovering, gives many a heartbreaking opportunity to choose the path we walk.

Tuesday Is Seniors' Discount Day

One of the fears we confront as we age is that of decrepitude. In a world that commodifies existence, we struggle to conceal any reduction in our utility. The weak do not produce; they become a burden to society and family. This commodification, endemic to a Western capitalist society, has precursors.

The use of the word "taxpayer" is our introduction to this way of thinking. "It's taxpayers' money. Hell, it's my money!" We've all heard that before. As a matter of fact, when I advise politicians on communications, I demand that they take "taxpayer" out of their speeches. What I object to in the constant use of this language within public discourse is the sheer selfishness of it. As we claw away at the public good, at our ability to care for and about each other, we are left with the naked and material walling-up of our lives. Private cars, homes, malls, communities. If we are merely taxpayers then we are positioned as customers who demand, but are often unwilling to pay for, the services that keep us safe and alive.

We become customers who have but one article of faith: our right to service. We demand better daycare but only if we have small children; better acute-care hospitals but only as we get older, or as our closest family members need one. We have forgotten to see ourselves as citizens. If taxpayers have rights, citizens have more. They have duties, rights and obligations. Are we obligated to each other? Do we step beyond our specific material lives to bend a knee toward each other and, as my Sabbath visitor said earlier, show that we are willing to engage in the spiritual task of walking each other home? Something has been profoundly attacked in this shrunken view of our lives. In my journey, it appears to be no small coincidence that our spiral into self-interest hit full acceleration when we decided that God was dead.

There, I said the word – the one that triggers so many thoughts and feelings. The G-word. So, for the sake of clarity I would like to tell you about the God that I *don't* believe in. That god is a man with a beard, sitting in a very nice chair. In his hand, and weighing on your conscience, is a naughty and nice list. That pediatric version of the divine is also known by another name – Santa Claus. In fact, this is the god that most of us now leave behind as we enter adolescence, never to engage with again.

It is said that we can choose to worship one god in many worlds or many gods in one. We have, as a culture I believe, chosen the latter. And what small gods do we now bow to? The latest movie star spewed out by the Hollywood hit-making machine, or an expensive shoemaker or fashion designer. Or someone who can kick a ball very hard while wearing shorts with an ad splattered across their jersey. These people will, for a brief time, become immortal.

Now imagine the distance between that small slice of idolization and what we see when we gaze through the Hubble Space Telescope at the literally millions of galaxies in constant and awe-inspiring flux. Imagine what it is to see God – not as a thing, a noun, but as a process. An unfolding, never-ceasing pulse of creation that animates every cell in our bodies and indeed every granular flake of stardust that we are, in the end, made of.

I often think of the life of stars. When they die and go supernova, the resulting enormous explosion forces nearby gases to come together and give birth to a new star. Life, death, birth. The cosmos is alive in ways we can't even imagine, and we are but a fantastic cellular spark in that majestic flow.

A priest named Matthew Fox was excommunicated from the Catholic Church in the early 1990s for saying that the church had devolved into "Jesus-ology": the worship not of Christ's consciousness but of the man, of Jesus. He argued that the faithful needed to reorient themselves back to a state of awe and wonder for creation itself. He calls it "Creation Spirituality," and his teachings have allowed me to see spirituality through a deeply ecumenical lens.

There is, in most religious talk, a not-so-subtle undertone of exclusion, a tribal vibe. I'll elaborate. At a workshop I conducted recently at a local synagogue, we were talking about the value proposition of being Jewish. What was in it for these people to identify as Jewish? At one point the dreaded "chosen people" label reared its misunderstood head. Some take the assignation as a sign of superiority, that as Jews, we have been singled out in some sort of divine lineup by the man behind the two-way mirror. "Him, he's the one." Weary but resigned to our fate, we now must serve a life sentence as beacons of light unto the world.

I addressed the woman who brought the issue to the group. "Perhaps," I offered, "we can look at this in a different way. You see, I identify with those who say that God's not Jewish, we're Jewish." She went quiet for a moment, appearing confused by what I had just said. "But he is," she finally said. We moved on, but two weeks later she came back to the group and said that she hadn't been able to stop thinking about what I'd said. I had challenged a fundamental belief in her, a definition of chosen people that she, as a convert to Judaism, had taken great comfort in.

What Fox and others have taught me is that there are many wells that lead to the one river. Spirituality is an exercise in profound intimacy – with others, with yourself and with the mystery that swirls around us and literally through the ever-living universe. Being Jewish speaks to my particular need to make sense of all this.

I identified as both a progressive and a religious person long before I was beset by heart disease and cancer. There was just one element missing. Death was, for me, no different than it is for most of us in this highly material and secular culture – a terrifying and downright rude assault on my march to forever. What I was beginning to realize is that I had assumed I was just going to skip right over the growing-older part. Like death, decrepitude was for my hundred-year-old grandmother or my liverspotted aunt. I was better than all that. I had recovered from angina and radiation. I was free to run back into the land of making money.

A year and a half earlier, I had been in a very different place. I was unhappy about my professional life, but personally rising to the challenge of starting a new, second family. I had been through many struggles: divorce and the pain that brought to my older children, as well as a gruelling work schedule – up at 4:30 a.m. to host a radio show, working on one of seventeen documentary programs and advising the fledgling Green Party of Canada on top of it all.

Through this all, a new and lovely ritual had emerged. With the first of my younger boys came a gift I have since come to cherish: the Sabbath. I had been working on a documentary series we called 5 *Seekers* and we were shooting out in Cortes Island, British Columbia, the home of the Hollyhock retreat. The point of the series was to witness and facilitate five seekers who had given up on religion but still found themselves spiritually wanting. One of the experiences we arranged for them was a visit with a woman on the island who every Friday night hosted an open Sabbath dinner.

Friday night is, of course, when Jews celebrate the arrival of Sabbath – *Shabbat* in Hebrew. In fact, it is the welcoming of the feminine divine, the *shechina*. What was interesting about this particular Sabbath is that the woman hosting was not Jewish. In fact, her home was a celebration of all spiritual paths. Walking around her living room was like moving through the stations of the cross except that at each station you were greeted by a different religious icon. Here was Buddha, next Ganesh from the Hindu faith, then Jesus and so on. She was specific in her choice of when to celebrate but deeply ecumenical in her choice of who would accompany her on this spiritual company.

The dinner was light and the company enjoyable, but what

I didn't realize at the time was that it would plant a seed in me that I would bring back to my home. I mentioned the dinner to my wife when I returned home and though she was raised in a secular home she agreed that we would start having similar Sabbath dinners at our house. Anyone was welcome. Some who attended we knew well, others barely at all and once in a while people would bring friends we had never even met.

The structure was simple: We spent time, and wine, with everyone flowing from the kitchen to the living room. Eventually we would move to the dinner table, and I would give a brief explanation of what the rituals of the Sabbath signify. I often referred to the writings of Abraham Joshua Heschel, whose book *The Sabbath* is concise, poetic and deeply resonant. He speaks of the notion that Jews create an architecture of faith that is fundamentally based not on brick and mortar – we are after all a deeply diasporic people, always moving from one land to another – but in time. There are six days when we are humans "doing" and only one where we are humans "being."

Sabbath is a time of reflection and connection, if we so choose. For the Orthodox, the strictures on works and labours of the home are severe. For most others, the observance diminishes to the point where, for many, the Sabbath is indistinguishable from any other day.

But imagine for a moment a world where we massively reduce our use of energy for a day. We keep a few lights on but give up running errands or scrolling on our phones. Maybe we take walks instead, or just spend the day connecting to each other and ourselves. I remember clearly when governments began promoting Sunday shopping. I had been disappointed. I thought of all those people who would now have to work on weekends; all those people who, without restraint, would now be shopping every day, all the time. There was no more day of rest. Shabbat is the greatest gift that the Jewish people have offered to the world. What a waste to toss it aside.

At our table, we light candles and then ask that everyone do a blessing. In this extemporaneous and often touching moment, I have seen husbands turn to wives and bless them for the love they bring even through the chaos of child-rearing or the pressures of their jobs. We have heard people bless their ailing parents or recently passed and much-beloved pets. There is something in the public proclamation of gratitude and in making sacred what would otherwise simply pass us by that transforms the feast every time.

This is different from a casual dinner party, with its bursts of small talk about this or that new TV show. Instead, dinner is a point of connection. For a moment we are stripped of the need to impress or entertain each other, and can instead speak of things that matter, both to us and to each other. You see, what Sabbath brings, what heart disease brings, what even cancer offers, is the deep knowledge that this is not a rehearsal. Life is not something that happens just as soon as we get these other bits out of the way. The day-to-day chore that doesn't quite satisfy; the daily routine of breakfast, lunch and "what's for dinner?" Life is only this moment, here, now.

When You Work You Always Have Tomorrow

I was sitting with a friend recently. Actually, he was more of a colleague. He'd had a distinguished career as a documentarian and we knew of each other in passing from my time at a public broadcaster. We met because I had passed him on a trail near my home in Hamilton one Sunday afternoon. I wasn't sure it was him as he passed – he looked so grey, and a little stooped. In fact, I thought he looked like an older version of the man I knew, not quite him but similar. He could just as easily have had the same thoughts about me with one added piece, given how my face, specifically my nose, has been altered by cancer, surgery and the passing of time.

I didn't say hello as we passed, but later I saw one of his posts on social media and messaged him to ask if he had been walking on the Cherry Hill trail that weekend. He had commented on a few of my Facebook posts recently so a bond, virtual and tenuous as it may have been, had formed. We arranged to get together for a coffee.

Upon meeting, we both unspooled our stories from the ten to fifteen years since we had last passed each other's desks. He had ventured out of the CBC and spent years making documentaries in the private sector. A challenging task at the best of times, but he had done okay. Lately, all of that had changed. He, like many others, had seen the documentary well run dry. But something else had also happened. His services were not sought after by those he had worked with before. Assumptions had been made that he was probably out of the game. After all he was sixty-seven – surely he was retired, hopping on cruise ships, playing the proverbial round of golf.

If you look at the magazines targeting seniors you will see a glut of ads for travel, resort living and the fantasy of the good life that awaits those in line to reap their just rewards. Metroland is the conglomerate responsible for buying up all the community-run newspapers in southern Ontario, where I live. They also bought a lot of other national papers. One of the publications they churn out in pursuit of advertising dollars carries the unfortunate title *Forever Young*. It's for the fifty-five-plus market. Framing people as young, and forever no less, is a form of gaslighting. "I'm getting older," we say. "No, you're not," we're told. You'll never get older, that would be awful. No, no, my friend, you are forever young.

As my colleague and I sat together that afternoon in the coffee shop, it became clear that he wasn't finished, that there was much he still wanted to say as a storyteller, but at sixty-seven he was finding it almost impossible to find his place in the public discourse. We paused for a moment, letting what we had shared sink in. Then he looked up from his coffee and said, "You know, when you work, you always have a tomorrow."

His words struck me. We gain so much meaning from our labours, whatever they are. Self-worth, human connection and the sense that we are needed – not just today but tomorrow as well. It is common to hear people complain about the busyness of their lives, the amount of things that have to get done at work and in the home. But there is more to this frenetic flow than we let on. There is validation: people are counting on me, they need this done, I matter.

It's the same rush that we get with every notification on our cellphones. The proof is in the moment, the one where we see that no one has sent a message of any kind to us in the last six hours. The pull to validation is so strong that we are actually willing to stake our lives on it. More people are now killed by distracted drivers, by people on their phones while driving, than by driving drunk. Work life is filled with connections that give us a tomorrow, but when that ends a vacuum is created, one that for many becomes a disheartening silence. We get a taste of its sting when we fall into any stretch of unemployment. Life throws down a gauntlet challenging our sense of who we are. The self-concept that we have built day by day through schooling, jobs and in some cases careers – perhaps the most freighted if not privileged version of our work self. Imagine having been a doctor, revered, seen as holding life and death in your hands. One day it's over and you no longer have an office to inhabit, a patient to see, a conference to attend. Your identity, no longer receiving its daily reinforcement, can go hungry as we retreat into the shadows of what we once were.

Recently, during an Age-ing to Sage-ing workshop I was conducting for men, this became a central theme. Each man in the group had been, or still was, a practising professional. Lawyers, financial advisors, doctors – they all had many things on their side. They were white, male and, yes, even though they had worked hard for the honour, they were privileged. One was in his seventies. He was a gentle, thoughtful man, but lately he had been annoyed at the frequency with which patients would say to him in the course of an examination, "So. When are you going to pack it in? Get out on the golf course?" I asked him what was upsetting about this almost daily topic of conversation, and he said that he had no intention of retiring and that he was tired of saying so. We talked a bit more and it became apparent that he resented how obvious it was to his patients that he was old. Many of his clientele had been with him, literally, for a lifetime. I asked if he intended on practising till he was either debilitated or dead. Without hesitation, he replied, yes. "What else would I do? I hate golf and I'm not much at sitting around the house." I was with him on the golf part but it seemed unfortunate that he saw his choices simply as what he had always been, doing what he had always done, or being no one. There is so much more that we can explore if we harvest our wisdom and find new purpose for our gifts.

But if we have not been spooning healthy dollops of soulful practice into our working lives, then we are orphaned as our work life fades or becomes smaller. My colleague in the café, the one who had once been needed and wanted in the documentary world, carried some of that sadness as we sat together sipping our coffees. We had both fallen silent as we reflected on how we had come to this point in our lives.

Since the age of thirty I have been looked upon as someone who's had a pretty good run of career luck. There have been some bumps along the way, but for a man who was spectacularly slothful throughout his youth I have grown quite a stiff backbone when it comes to work. Skills that emerged in my chaotic twenties became powerful tools for career advancement and survival as the years marched on.

The first leg of the career journey requires throwing a saddle over your ego, that part of you responsible for creating your identity and sense of self-worth, and taking it for a ride. A wild ride for me at times. The Christian mystic Richard Rohr speaks at length about the place of ego in our spiritual lives. Like others, he offers that we must find the proper place for ego-driven choices as we walk the spiritual path. Ideally, if I understand him correctly, we must learn to let go of the construction of personality, which is the busy work of ego, and be available to the profound and simple power of what is.

Throughout my working life I have been struck by the subtle but persistent ambience of fear that swirls around us in the workplace. Imagine a tank filled not with piranha or sharks (the common metaphorical props used to describe the denizens of the office deep), but well-dressed, late-working schools of pufferfish showing all those around them that they have "it" under control – oh, and by the way, if you try to touch them as they climb the career ladder, you'll die. As I age, I have grown more tender in my feelings about the workplace. Sad, really, for all the ideas that fell on deaf ears, those unused gifts.

Every place I have worked has erred on the side of operational competence. Being Canadian, a hockey image comes to mind. To paraphrase the Great One, Wayne Gretzky: You have to skate to where the puck is going, not where it is. I'm not deriding the need to get things done; I'm speaking about something else – the skill of workplace levitation. Floating above the situational imperatives just long enough to bring a new perspective, so that we can imagine what might come next. But what is the fuel that will help us achieve that altitude?

I have been lucky enough in recent years to have been schooled in creative problem-solving methodologies through a curriculum devised by SUNY at Buffalo State College. The emphasis, in a nutshell, is deferring judgment and generating a quantity of ideas in a safe and often joyful workshop environment. Convergent tools are provided to help narrow down choices and refine outcomes, but the key for me is the deferring of judgment. Being free to generate a quantity of ideas. In fact, their research shows that many of the best ideas happen in the time after we think we have exhausted the pool of ideas that we have been drawing on.

This dovetails nicely with the work I have done to become an ordained spiritual director. There we were asked to allow workshop partners, or a co-worker in a meeting for that matter, to take the risk of being brave, of being heard. How many times have we been asked in a meeting to "blue sky it"? A ridiculous request when all hierarchies of organizational life are rigid and intact. All done with the boss in the room, looking for a near-term solution with no iterative process involved. We talk ad nauseam of innovation in the new millennia, but we do not allow for it to flourish. We are too timid. Innovation requires courage. My definition is simple: Innovation is subversion looking for respect. Innovation is the party crasher that says we need a truly novel solution to an existing problem. Creativity is the jet fuel that can bring these soulful ways of thinking out to the greater benefit of the organization and ourselves. How many dreams, ideas and easy fixes are lying dormant in the people who work around and with us?

The belief for many is that creativity, and the soulful opening that it brings, is the domain of a few "creatives" that are hired to live in that blue sky that everyone seems to think is swirling above them somewhere, just out of reach. Creativity, compassion and confidence are the materials that allow us to build our futures. They do not belong to a select few. They are obvious in the eyes of every child that is given a chance to be heard, loved and respected.

Sir Ken Robinson, the educator and king of creativity, describes a slow smothering of the creative spark in our education culture. You can see it when you walk through an elementary school. In the beginning, our beginnings, as it were, we have walls covered with absurdly colourful images, crafts everywhere. Singing and learning together in a close-knit group takes place in classrooms filled with love and care. When kids are young, the magic in their eyes can soften even the most utilitarian of hearts. As they age, we bring more pressure to bear on them. They must steel themselves to take on a world that has lost its magic, has tamed its spirit with the promise of material reward. The children's pictures come down and are replaced by text-driven narratives.

From there we move on to deliverables to illustrate competence and the ability to take in, remember and deliver mostly predetermined outcomes. Children become good, I might suggest, at showing up, shutting up and performing. I was conducting a creativity workshop where the group, educators mostly, spoke about how the system is killing the creativity of their children. But something felt wrong. I offered that it was not the system but all of us in the room that were the perpetrators of this creativity-killing. In our rush to inoculate our children from the vagaries of the world, we demanded that they gain the hard skills that we could use and take comfort in. The B+ in math, the 90 percent in chemistry. If it's English, history or, heaven forfend, art then the prize is less, but it's still better than nothing. We do not encourage the skills that allow us to think critically about the world we must live in. The soft skills of team building and interpersonal relationships are done off to the side of the desk, so to speak.

Creativity is considered frivolous because it is often off point, disruptive, mischievous. It challenges conventionality. In the Jewish tradition, this is an essential part of learning. Students are set in pairs, given a piece of sacred text and then told to dissect, defend and listen to alternative ways of seeing the events and actions described therein. Which gives us the stereotype of the Jewish scholar who posits a point of view and then pauses for a second before saying, "On the other hand." This can go on, and has, for millennia.

It's a good thing when we are pondering the meaning of life. In our modern secular world, we have given up on the ambiguity that this line of inquiry brings. Save for occasional pockets of brave thinking, we are enraptured with rationality. There is a Chinese proverb that states, and I'm paraphrasing here, "To be uncertain is uncomfortable. To be certain is ridiculous." We have chosen to be certain. I never felt this more acutely than when I worked as a political consultant and communications director. Each of the political parties formed into tight, aggressive clusters. And from within, the party's new entities were always forming and reforming, mostly driven by the urge to power. If you took their political platforms and drew connective lines between policy proposals you would find many points of connection and convergence. Yet, if you asked their various members – and it seemed the lower you went in their ability to wield influence and real power, the more strongly they held to this way of being – they puffed out their chests and declared that they and they alone were absolutely right and the other political amalgams were just dead wrong.

This binary nonsense, rooted in patriarchal systems of dominance and victory, has done great damage to our civil society. Imagine if political parties were dissolved and re-localized representations emerged. Imagine a decentralized way forward on so many fronts. Scale breeds insensitivity, risk adversity and simplistic answers to complex human problems. As you can imagine, my lack of fealty to the cause was considered suspect at best. It was a healthy hangover from my journalistic life.

How many times have you heard someone say the words "soul sucking" when describing their work life? I often use this story to illustrate the problem. You're driving to work, and on the radio you hear one of those songs. I'll say it's Heart doing their cover of "Stairway to Heaven." By the time the choir kicks in behind the lead singer's balls-out vocals, you're this close to official headbanger status. You arrive at the staff parking lot, turn off the car right at the top of the guitar solo and turn to your other self. "Right, you stay here in the car. I'm going in." For many, work consumes most of our waking hours. But how much of ourselves do we take though those doors? How spiritually and psychologically safe do we feel?

When the meeting is over, you walk by a field of desks on the way back to your office, catching glimpses of a family photo here or the memento from an all-too-brief vacation there. Artifacts of a life outside this place. Of why we came here – to provide. But in many cases, there is a spiritual deficit at play, and the cost-benefit analysis shows that what we lose is the collective genius that sits out in the parking lot, waiting for our return. In a time when utility trumps value, we are often asked only for our operational best. Ideation is reserved for those spasmodic boardroom meetings where we are asked to digest and decide on the way forward.

In an environment where risk can be career limiting, not much can come of the request that we "think big." As for our wisdom, well that's often met with a youthful eye roll.

So, what is the status of the older person in the workplace? Seeing my work dissolve before my eyes, I began to wrestle with this question for the first time. If we are to live longer and healthier, intent not on retiring but on inspiring, how do we carve out a new space for ourselves? A third space where organizations and businesses employ elders who can mentor, apply well-refined experience and abilities, and use integrated thinking skills that neuroscience has proven improve with age. How can we bring our wisdom to the table? This is not a case for being charitable and giving a former employee a little office nearby out of pity, or an academic an emeritus shingle to hang on an empty office door. This is about rethinking how we can truly leverage institutional memory, sage advice and intergenerational contact. I imagine that with less ego and more soulfulness, elders will have a great deal to contribute, should they so desire. At the senior level, yes, but also in the workaday world were most of us toil away.

These spiritual black holes have their parallels in the world of religion as well. As we cling to tradition, we devolve into a concrete-like adherence to hollowed-out rituals. We take refuge in beliefs and leave the risk of faith out in the parking lot. After all, they don't call it a leap of faith for nothing. I know it's hard to bounce around like this but stay with me – and try not to think of Charlton Heston while I share this bible story with you. So, Moses is standing with the Hebrews and those who decided to join them on their exodus to freedom. In front of them is the Red Sea, but fast approaching to their rear is the pharaoh's mighty army led by Yul Brynner – I mean Ramses II. Moses is begging God for guidance. "What do I do? The Egyptians are coming and they will surely slaughter us all. There is no escape. We have our backs to the sea." While Moses is begging/praying, one of the elders – a relative in fact – Nachshon, has either jumped or been pushed into the sea. I love the ambiguity of that. If he was pushed then this is all an accident; if he leapt then his actions are noble. For me, it doesn't matter either way, because it's what he does next that's important. You see, sometimes we need a push, and sometimes we just say to hell with it and jump. See *Butch Cassidy and the Sundance Kid* for further proof.

What Nachshon does next is walk. The water rises to his knees and he keeps going; his hips feel the splash of cold salt water and he keeps walking. Meanwhile Moses hears the voice within: "What are you doing grovelling before me in your fear?

Look at what Nachshon is doing." By now Nachshon is almost completely submerged, but he keeps on walking. Moses takes his staff and leads the people into the roiling waters. The seas part, and in overcoming their fears they catch a glimpse of freedom.

I'm not a literalist in any way. I have no need to prove that the event took place at a low tide, that the escape was purely at the whim of nature. To me the pharaoh is our inner oppressor, Egypt the interior landscape that keeps us enslaved and the leap that Nachshon takes is the difference between cowering at our desks or taking the chance of bringing ourselves – all of ourselves – to what we do. The crisis is one of leadership, and even though their cages are gilded the enslavement can be, and mostly is, just as real for those that climb the ladder of career. This lack of spirit wears on us as we pass the years enmeshed in work cultures that treat us all as temporarily essential. As we age in our workplaces, the spiritual aspects of our efforts yearn for expression. We have realized that there is not much from our labours that will live on once we leave our work behind, and more often than not we leave work with a whimper and not a bang.

There is something sad about the notice that flashes on our shared screens. "Please join me (fill in middle management/ supervisor's name) as we get together and wish (employee with a long and loyal work history) a hearty congratulations as he/ she moves on to new and exciting adventures." Well-meaning colleagues mill about munching on a pizza slice, give the retiree a pat on the back and say, "Hey, keep in touch." You know that in almost every case they won't. It's not their fault, it's just that once you're gone, you're out of the daily flow. Proximity breeds friendship, distance the opposite.

But what happens to all the wisdom and hard-earned experience that person takes with them? It just disappears like sand passing through the hands of those that follow. Without an elder culture we have no way of turning to these men and women for advice. Imagine if we gathered in what organizations like Changing World call "Career Legacy Circles." Imagine creating a meaningful purpose and eventual exit for those who age in work – one that brings dignity and consciousness to the process instead of leaving us each to mourn the passing of a career cycle alone, drowning in a sea of well-meaning platitudes. Career Legacy Circles bring together six to twelve people in the later stages of their active working lives, and they meet over a two-to-four-week period for three hours at a time. First, they share a retrospective of their individual career journeys with each other. Bringing voice to their experiences. Then they create a prospective for a meaningful career exit and finish with an action plan for completing what needs to be done within the organization before they go.

I remember when I left Canada's national broadcaster after twenty-one years of radio and television broadcasting. The last day was so hollow and devoid of meaning. I fault no one. I quietly packed up a few boxes to take home, brought the car around to an illegal parking spot, then rushed up the elevators to grab my box of paper memories, my clumsy drafting table and chair, and an old broken-down desktop computer that they charged me fifty dollars to take with me. There was no pizza, no pat on the back and certainly no legacy circle.

I had just reached a stage where I had something of value to share as a mentor to the next generation of communicators, and I had instead been deemed surplus. I know, I had a long run in a precarious business, but isn't all work precarious, all loyalty thinned out and disposable?

Extra, Extra, Read All About It!

My sister is really smart. Lots of degrees, lots of opinions. While I was slipping down the greasy pole of showbiz, more out of choice than pressure, she had enrolled in yet another academic program. This time it was the Journalism school at Ryerson Polytechnic University, now Ryerson University. I thought nothing of it until one day when I was sitting in my bathrobe on the couch of a second-floor apartment that I shared with several acting friends in downtown Toronto. Back then actors could actually live downtown without starving.

So there I was, in my bathrobe, smoking hash, having slept till noon. I turned on the TV and watched one of Canada's first news magazine shows for a lunchtime crowd. I was stoned, the anchor was stone-faced. As he read, I thought to myself that any half-decent actor could do his job. It's all in the read. I started to wonder how much he made. Back then I thought, like most people would, that he must be making a mint. Not so much, I found out later. I remembered my sister and her studies. I called her up and asked what she thought of J-school, as they called it. I also asked if I could tag along to one of her classes. She said she'd ask.

Luckily, her prof said yes. Her name was Joan Donaldson and a few years later she would help launch Canada's first all-news network, Newsworld. One day, while she was leaving the CBC building in Montreal, she stepped off a curb and was hit by a bike courier. She suffered severe brain damage and later died from her injuries. One minute, in one day, on a city street and regardless of where we are off to, it's over. It makes you wonder why. But over the years of my spiritual hunt I've found it is not the answer that satisfies me, it's refining the questions.

I sat in Ms. Donaldson's class that day and listened as the students discussed current events. I was twenty-seven and found the conversation fascinating. I had, since the last day of my own schooling, soaked up the politics of development, the history of the twentieth century and the realpolitik of the Cold War and the Holocaust. This conversation felt right.

I applied to the program with help from my sister and got in. I was at that time living with the woman who would become my wife in a few years. I was feeling different, free from all that I had thought I was destined to be. My friends from the comedy and acting worlds just shook their heads. As far as they were considered, I was turning my back on both them and my true self. But I wasn't.

My first-year broadcast teacher would steer me to my first radio job and become a friend. He had already made a name for himself as the wunderkind of CBC radio. Executive producer of the flagship documentary program *Sunday Morning*, and now a regular contributor to the never to be surpassed *Morningside* with Peter Gzowski. His name was Stuart McLean. Stuart would go on to reinvent himself as the national storyteller, capturing a small-town sensibility with stories carefully refined by his co-writer, Meg Masters. They were tales filled with laughter, love and the sweet nostalgia for main street Canada. A more innocent time, they say, provided, that is, you were white and Christian.

Stuart and I even created a Christmas TV special together years later. We would drive the hour and a half to Belleville from Toronto to shoot, reminiscing along the way. When I heard that he had contracted a cancer and that it wasn't going well, it broke my heart. I remember going to see him perform in Brantford, Ontario, before we began production on the special. I wanted to be inside the magic he created up onstage. That night there was a driving snowstorm. The roads were treacherous, but the beautiful old theatre, a remnant of the old vaudeville touring days, was packed. Watching him up there was like witnessing a love affair. We could all forget our troubles; he was leading us to a part of our better selves, and we went willingly. Before turning to leave, our collars turned up to face that harsh and snowy night, we smiled at each other. Stuart McLean was a good man.

I loved J-school. I was older, I knew why I was there and I was discovering the beautiful world of storytelling through radio and television – no longer a last call actor or a so-so comedian but a critically thinking and creative journalist. There were some good teachers and some bad. I would occasionally hear the phrase "Out in the real world," a term weaponized by many an instructor. "Now folks in the real world, they won't stand for the kind of crap you churned out today, you'll be out on your ass in a second."

One day I couldn't take any more. I was eight or nine years older than my classmates and had actually lived "in the real world." "Excuse me," I said, not waiting to be acknowledged. "I've been in the real world and it's not nearly as awful as you keep telling us it will be." My point was not taken, nor was it appreciated. I continued, "There's lots of crappy work and low standards out there, don't worry we'll find something."

I had one English prof who insisted that Canadian humorist and icon Stephen Leacock wasn't funny. He was telling us, by the way, not putting it out there for discussion. Once again, I flexed my mature student muscle. Why? For one thing, when you are a mature student you are more aware that in post-secondary education, the class offered is a product for which hundreds, if not thousands, of dollars must be paid – by you. Secondly, I had arrived relatively free of the accumulated freight of eighteen continuous years of institutional pedagogy. Those around me were fresh-faced and ready to do whatever the sage on the stage asked of them. Some were quite adept at gaming the system for ultimate advantage while some were not equipped with, or cared to employ, the self-protecting powers of critical thinking. They had simply not been rewarded for that skill.

I have worked on many news and current affairs programs as well as in government, politics and post-secondary environments. The ability for people in those environments to think cynically – you know, the eye wink, "I know what's going on but I'm above it" approach – is common currency. Critical thinking, on the other hand, is often absent.

In fact, as I said before, critical thinking and robust creativity are discouraged throughout society. Phrases like "pie in the sky," "out of the box" and "left field" all signal disruption of the various organizations and their technocratic approach. If you want to make a lot of money as a consultant to these lumbering corporate middleweights best to come armed with PowerPoints, Venn diagrams and the certainty of numerical projections. No room for mystery or chance. But let's get back to English class.

So there I am with this sage on the stage telling me and my classmates that Leacock isn't funny. I disagreed. I asked if I could illustrate my point by reading a passage. I read, the class laughed at the precise moment Leacock had intended and the teacher's face reddened. He asked me as we were leaving if we could have a word. He offered me a deal: I could write the essays and exam, but he would do me a favour and not require me to attend lectures anymore. I accepted. I shouldn't have. I should have stayed and modelled a different approach to the great power he held in such a small hand.

It's strange how we grasp for certainty as we stumble through this life. I was going to be an actor, I could only be funny, I was fat, I was good looking. The Buddhist notion of suffering the state that we inhabit as humans is predicated on the urge to cling and grasp. We crave control. What that thinking does, however, is make me unaware of what is right in front of me. Case in point, let's look at radio. Besides wandering into a radio station at the University of Alberta once, which had been a great moment really, I had never thought about radio. I asked, out of the blue, if I could go on the air. The guy said sure, come back Tuesday at lunch, they had an hour to fill. And I did. I had no training, no clue really about how to cue up a record beyond a station manager showing me once. I was terrified. I wanted to cling to his leg and be dragged out of the studio never to return, but I didn't. Instead I picked a seventeen-minute song by Perth County Conspiracy – there were a lot of seventeen-minute songs back then – to give myself the time to figure out what the hell to do. I survived, and vowed never to try that again.

But here I was at the Ryerson radio station CKLN. Anton Leo, one of my closest friends from Yuk Yuk's who always had a much more level head than I, was the station manager. I begged him for a job that I made up on the spot. I wanted to be the news director. There was no news director. Hell, there was no news on the station. It was a hodgepodge of reggae, punk, far-out morning jazz, emerging hip hop and old fart rock.

Out of nowhere I designed a five-morning-a-week magazine show with headlines, interviews and editorials for anyone who wanted to be on air. I hosted one day of programming as well. My mind was blown. I had no idea that speaking into that microphone would the beginning of a lifelong love affair with radio. The intimacy, the way that the listener had to engage and imagine . . . The description Marshall McLuhan gave radio was perfect. It was a hot medium. TV was and still is a cold medium – you are passive, receiving; it's the perfect selling tool. Radio, particularly public and not-for-profit radio, is none of that. By now I was listening to Peter Gzowski every morning on *Morningside*. He was the epitome of a current affairs magazine host. In my opinion, he has no peer when it came to bringing the nation into a small and intimate space, and drawing the best out of each and every guest. Prime ministers, k.d. lang, orphaned children, coal miners, pundits – he was the ultimate tour guide.

I made up my mind: I wanted to work at the CBC. I wanted to work in radio. I wanted to dive into the real issues of the day. The class clown would have to take a supporting role from here on out. Life was changing. I didn't realize it, but I would become the kind of person who thrived in reinvention.

I was two years into the three-year program at Ryerson, approaching thirty and wanting to get married to my partner and have kids. Enter Stuart McLean, stage left. "You know, Ralph, I've been thinking that you really don't need to be here. There's a job available out at CBC Winnipeg for a current affairs researcher working on the morning drive-home shows." "But I still have a year to go, and they want me to be the editor of the *Ryersonian* in first term next year," I said. I had always sucked at school and now, for once, I was actually doing well. Stuart persisted. He gave me the contact info and I called to make an appointment.

Winnipeg. What did I know about Winnipeg? Really cold, middle of nowhere and half my friends had come to Toronto to get out of there. When I told one of them that I was applying for a job in Winnipeg, they said, "You're going the wrong way."

I began to prepare. First, I cold-called a producer there and asked how they format their interviews. They started with a focus statement – why you're interviewing this person – then an intro paragraph for the host and five questions. Those usually started with a why: "Why did you take on this project?"

I threw myself at the task. Someone, I can't remember who, got me access to the CBC research library. There was no Internet, no Google back then, just microfiche and hard copies of newspapers from around the country and the rest of the world. I scoured the back editions of the *Winnipeg Free Press*. This was real and I wanted to be totally prepared. I happen to have a neurodiverse brain, though I grew up with no label for that. I was just "bored" in school, disruptive, unable at times to pay attention to details. Today with two if not three of my children living with the same obstacles, I can tell them, I'm with you. I have ADHD, too.

But this time I was ready to plow through, to be thorough. I collected eighteen stories. The term for these focus, intro questions and guest scripts was a "Green." I went to the interview, spent the entire time talking story ideas and got a call soon after offering me the Winnipeg job. It was full time, twenty-three thousand dollars a year! I paid one of my ex-Winnipeg friends $450 for his geriatric blue Volvo and packed the wheezing old beater to the gunnels with everything from clothes to records and started off by myself on the two-day drive the Peg.

Two hours out of Toronto I heard a bang and then the flip-flop of rubber as the car starting grinding to the right. I pulled over. I was already terrified of what I had just committed to – a straight job in a city I didn't know, and the real possibility that I was going to screw this up. Hell, I didn't even have a degree to show for all my J-school efforts. So there I was, staring at a flat tire on the side of the road on the way to the Trans-Canada Highway. I rummaged through the trunk not knowing if I even had a spare tire let alone the tools to make the change. I found the thingamabob that loosens the nuts. I thought, okay you can probably do this. I couldn't. No matter how hard I tried I couldn't move the nut.

All of a sudden, I looked up and there was a bear of a man standing on the shoulder. I hadn't even noticed that someone had driven up behind me and stopped. He had a thick French accent and an even thicker beard and belly. "Need some 'elp?" he said. Years later, while I was training to become a spiritual director, I would be asked to write a paper on angels. I demurred, telling the rabbi teaching the course that I really couldn't relate to the idea of winged do-gooders or even do-badders. In response, the rabbi led me through a guided meditation, and I realized that what she was talking about was more metaphorical. Angel energies appear at different times and through different channels in your life. I thought about my guardian angels. My father, my old best friend, both dead. I remembered this burly and kind man who knelt down and, with a mighty turn of the wrench, loosened the bolts, put on the service tire and lowered the jack. All without an agenda. Just because I was on the side of the highway and he could help.

The minute before he arrived, I was already thinking that this whole Winnipeg thing had been a huge mistake. The night before, my partner and I had thrown a big bon voyage party for all our showbiz friends. I had wondered how in hell could I turn my tail between my ambitious legs and admit defeat. Instead, a guardian angel had arrived and pushed me a little further from my past life and into the one that awaited me.

I got a new tire in Gogama, where the mechanic also told me that my brakes were close to shot, but I had no money to do anything about that. The radio was dead so I perched my Walkman on the dash with two seriously chintzy little speakers attached, and on day two I drove for fifteen hours straight. At the border between Ontario and Manitoba, everything changed. As I listened to the CBC, the rugged lake region of Kenora gave way to the flattest land I had ever seen. The sky was like an upside-down ocean of blue with crested clouds like whitecaps floating above me. I arrived at a friend's apartment.

They were out of town, but the landlady saw me pull up and asked if I was staying with Charlie and Betty. She handed me the key to their place. I dragged my belongings in, minus two milk cartons of records I had left on the side of the road somewhere round Lake Superior. I figured less weight might mean I could still stop suddenly even with worn-out brake pads.

I had a hot bath, sat down and watched a CFL football game. I don't remember who played, I just sat and watched. It was Saturday night. By Monday I would be starting at the CBC building on Portage Avenue.

I spent my thirties and forties working at the CBC. I always tell people that it was like being in a candy store – I could try a little of this and a little of that. Move between current affairs and variety, TV and radio. I worked on contract the whole time. Year after year that made me have to think of what I could do next.

I have seen my country and fallen in love with it. We, unlike much of the "Old World," do not have seven-hundred-year-old churches. Our cathedrals are made of fir and redwood. Our monuments are of towering granite and ocean-chiselled sandstone. We scatter along the southern border most often, and live an impossible dream of nationhood. Thousands of kilometres separate our coasts. Language, geography and powerful regions crush together to make a place we can't define but know is ours the minute we leave it for work or pleasure.

From that first day in Winnipeg, pitching stories for the morning information radio program, to my last day, packing up my office with no fanfare or goodbye, I had the privilege of giving voice and my life's energy to telling the Canadian story.

They say that youth is wasted on the young. I don't think so. What I do know is that my young journey was very much fuelled by a cocktail of ambition, ego, success and heartbreak. I spent two years in Winnipeg. Our first child was born there. My first eight months I was a current affairs researcher booking guests, cigarette in hand, for the local drive shows. Then I was host of the late-night weekend FM show *Nightlines*. My producer was Ross Porter. We had a blast staying up till 3:00 a.m. each weekend night playing true FM setlists. Ross had an encyclopedic music mind and exquisite taste in many genres but particularly in jazz. We would remain friends for a long time.

But Winnipeg was not home. I remember being in the parking lot at Polo Park mall and, looking up, thinking I'd recognized someone. "What am I thinking, I don't know anyone here." I had to get home. Remember Anton, the station manager at CKLN? The one I had started with at Yuk Yuk's? While I was burrowing away on the Prairies, he had landed a job at CBC trying to get all the afternoon shows to drag themselves musically into the 1980s. It was not that much fun, with some schmuck from head office in Toronto telling you to play a little more Tears for Fears and a lot less Celtic folk.

As I yearned for home, Anton found his way into a show called *Prime Time*. It was brand new and the host and the producer weren't gelling. He tipped me off that change might be afoot. I started contributing; I focused on finding a way in, and lo and behold I was offered the job. Stand-up had been a low-rent jungle and I was not cut out for the itinerant life it offered. Nightclub performing could kill any marriage, and poverty held no romantic interest for me. I wanted to be creative every day and witness the fruits of that labour. I was on my way. Anton, with his own illustrious career and a heart of gold, and I lunched together most days over the next eighteen years at CBC. My friend, Anton, was the only thing that I truly missed as I walked out the door after two decades. We don't see each other enough.

Career climbing is hard and sometimes unfeeling work. I regret not having enough kindness and certainly not enough wisdom to cherish my opportunities or the people who helped me along the way.

When Anton and I revamped *Prime Time,* we got in touch with Paul K. Willis, one of our friends from my stand-up days. He and his comedic partner were known as La Troupe Grotesque. Man, could he write funny. He became our show announcer, and his openings were wonderful. Sadly, he passed many years ago and I still miss him. My first interview for the show was with legendary actor Gordon Pinsent. He was a great talker and his skill made me look good – it was a nice way to start.

Radio was good to me. We worked out of the old radio building on Jarvis Street, where there were no elevators and, occasionally, we found mice in the desk drawers. But at least the windows opened and there were no security gauntlets to navigate. Unfortunately, it was there that security became a thing. One weekend, Tom Shipton, who was the producer for the *Royal Canadian Air Farce,* was busy getting his show together for air when he noticed someone strange walking around in the building. He asked if he could help and the man became evasive. Tom followed him, and eventually the man lashed out and then ran out of the building. After that there was a guard in the parking lot making sure you had ID. It felt then like a subtle but real loss of innocence. The Jarvis Street building was also where I first met the legendary Peter Mansbridge. At the time he drove a flashy Toyota sports car and was the anchor-in-waiting as Knowlton Nash wound down his tenure.

Peter reached out after I had done something that was, shall we say, unusual. The Winnipeg police had notified me that I had hundreds of dollars in unpaid parking tickets. Let's just say accumulating those violations was a family affair. I offered a novel solution to the problem – I would headline for a week at the Winnipeg Yuk Yuk's with all proceeds going to the Winnipeg Police parking tags office. Somehow the Canadian Press wire service got hold of the story and it went old-school viral, appearing in papers around the country. When I came back from the show, I was seated with Peter at a luncheon. He was tickled by the spirit of the tale, and I was flattered that he was even talking to me.

My next step was a big switch. I moved from *Prime Time* and radio to Canada's number one daytime TV magazine show, *Midday*. The show was well funded and had a global canvas – the first Gulf War, the Oka Crisis, the Meech Lake and Charlottetown Accords. My days were filled with interviewing and research, and my co-host, Valerie Pringle, was a wonderful person and a real mentor. She was authentic, intelligent and fun.

Valerie was the best mentor I could have asked for. Smart, witty and generous. Our chemistry was there from day one. She would joke to anyone coming in for an interview, "This is Ralph, he's about to tell you that he's a Spanish Moroccan Jew." She was, sadly, right. We travelled the country going to Smithers, BC; Prince Edward Island; Iqaluit up in Nunavut – you name it and we went there. In studio, the world came to us.

I love shows that are done in a magazine-style format. You get a whole range of topics – finance ministers after a budget, the Barenaked Ladies before anyone really knew who they were. One guest I will always remember was American blues and jazz icon Eartha Kitt. I had interviewed her in London, England, for my previous show, *Prime Time*. We were there for a two-week recording spree and in that time spoke with Pierce Brosnan, 10cc partners Godley & Creme, Richard Branson on his boathouse parked in a murky canal. Ms. Kitt came to our CBC radio studio in downtown London. On the way there, she had noticed a houseplant outside a producer's office. She immediately took out a pair of scissors and proceeded to give the shrub a less-than-gentle haircut. I was dumbfounded and didn't know what to say or do. Having finished her trim, she marched by me and into the studio. There she sat like a sphinx, staring off into the distance until the moment I finished the introduction. I said hello and she lit up with a ten-thousand-volt smile and engaged in deep eye contact. Interview over, I ushered her out, hoping she would wreak no more havoc. The producer had returned from lunch by the time I came back. She, well, she was freaking out. (The plant made the *Daily Mail*.)

Flash forward to the *Midday* set. Ms. Kitt was in town on a promotional tour. I walked into the makeup room. This time I was going to have none of her gamesmanship. She wore a stylish purple scarf wrapped around her head and was, once again, sitting sphinx-like. "Hi, Eartha," I said as I approached, "don't know if you remember me but we spoke in London once a little while back. You butchered a plant. It made the *Daily Mail*. No plants out on set today though, sorry. Anyway, I'll see you out there in about ten minutes."

Much of what we did on *Midday* was taped during the morning for a hard deadline of 11:00 a.m. to air in the Maritimes. Eartha sat down during pre-tape. I introduced her, and she leaned toward me on the couch and literally cooed, "I like you." She said something then about men. Not sure what but I responded, asking what she thought of men. There was a bowl of clear marbles on the coffee table in front of us. She dug into them and, holding them above the glass-top table, said, "Men are like water, they just pass through your hands." At this point she released the cascade of clear glass marbles onto the plate glass top. They crashed down, almost breaking the surface. She smiled.

But I had learned something by the time of that second interview with Ms. Kitt. Just like in stand-up, you have to make the performance space your own. Journalists hate admitting that there is an element of theatre in their craft, but there is. I remember sitting on set one day with one of our senior producers who was filling in for Valerie. I said that we were doing theatre in a way. She was mortified and insisted that we weren't. Now don't get me wrong, I'm not saying that she and I did not diligently do our research and employ, to the best of our abilities, the highest journalistic standards. I was saying that every story has to be sold. Every show implores you to stay tuned, to be loyal. To engage emotionally. Everyone says, "Don't go away, we'll be right back." To prove my point, I asked my producer what she thought our opening theme and credits were designed to do. I belted out the tune: "ba da da dada dum da da dah!" Cue the big-voiced announcer, *Midday* – with Valerie Pringle and Ralph Benmergui. Cut from the overhead two shot to a single of Valerie as she reads from the prompter. Cut to Ralph as he pivots toward camera with the green screen behind him. Music out. Did I take my responsibility to be well read and thorough seriously? Yes. Did I have on a ton of hairspray and makeup to make me look less cadaverous? Also yes.

Back to Eartha. I thanked her at the end of the interview and she flashed me that ten-thousand-volt smile. I had taken a bit of my stand-up life and repurposed it for my next as interviewer and host.

I'll share two more quick stories of my time on *Midday*, which was a great show to work on. One involves the great Vegas illusionist act Penn & Teller. Penn Jillette did all the talking, with Teller being the Harpo Marx of the duo – silent and elf-like. While we were on the couch – all entertainment in-studio guests were seated on the couch – and I was talking to Penn, Teller got up and started poking at the fake city skyline in the flat behind us. It was kind of funny. He was pointing out the artificial ambience of the set. When he sat down again, I figured I'd ask him a question to see how he would respond. "You're kind of the Harpo in this act, right?" I asked. Teller looked insulted and proceeded to pick up a full glass from that same coffee table and throw it in my face. He missed my face but did nail the shirt and tie. My only thought was whether or not my lapel microphone still worked. I could hear it in my earpiece so I carried on. Having been a stand-up I got what he was trying to do. I also knew, like he did, that it hadn't turned out to be that funny. I finished the interview, and as soon as the floor director said, "And we're off," Teller jumped up and said, "I am so sorry, really, I'll buy you a new shirt, can I get you a tie?" "No problem. I get what you were after there," I said. My executive producer happened to be up in the control room at the time. She was angry. I headed her off before she could say anything. "Susanne," I said, "they didn't mean anything by it. He was just trying it out. Believe me, there will be people who will see that and remember for the rest of their lives." She cooled down and they left, a little bit sheepish. Television is a medium of moments and emotions.

The last story involves the chairman of the CBC at the time, the famed and tough-minded broadcaster Patrick Watson. The government of the day under Conservative prime minister Brian Mulroney had just announced devastating cuts of $108 million to the annual budget of the CBC. I was called at home to say that we had an early afternoon "double-ender" with Watson. A double-ender was when the guest had a camera crew and a telex available to them. The crew would shoot the guest's answers with professional visuals and sound. The guest would hear you through an earphone. In this case, I was on the phone from home, having by then finished both taping and the story meeting. I had a four-year-old downstairs, so I kept him busy and went up and closed the bedroom door so as not to be interrupted. Watson was truly a gifted broadcaster, having hosted and revolutionized current affairs television with the seminal *This Hour Has Seven Days*. He asked tough questions. We began, and I asked at some point if he felt comfortable going along with these drastic cuts, which would see regional TV and radio taking the brunt of the fiscal blow. He shot back, saying, "Well, would you rather they have some political hack in this job?" At this point my son was banging on the door. I persevered: "Well, aren't you in danger of becoming a political hack by going along?" Watson exploded, and I suddenly had an angry child in the backroom and an angrier chairman of the broadcaster that employed me on the phone. "Benmergui, you are subject to the laws of libel, calling me a political hack." I don't remember much else of the interview after that. I hung up feeling a combination of excited and fearful. I had stood up to an uber boss, and it would be on national television the next day.

Remember I spoke about the theatre of journalism? Well, here's the perfect example. The next day I had to go on set and re-enact the interview so that they could record me in studio as if it were live. I had a choice to make. I knew what Mr. Watson was going to say. I could have added a good dollop of calm and arrogance that would make me look good and him look even worse. I decided to do something else. I employed what little genuine acting skill I could still muster and became totally present to what was in front of me, though I was actually as scared and exhilarated as I had been the day before. Propelled by the knowledge that what was said was going out to the entire country, I didn't need to fake anything. In a double-ender, when you start talking, the floor director counts you down with hand signals so that you can fit your comments and questions into a hard hole in the tape, as they say.

One thing did bother me. The producer had decided to bury the interview at the bottom of the hour. I knew they had dynamite on their hands, given the dynamics of the situation, but they were too scared to lead with it. Once it was done, I started getting calls from people. The one that meant the most was from the head of both our program and *The Journal* with Barbara Frum, Mark Starowicz. He congratulated me and said he was proud. Even the head of current affairs liked it. It was he who told my executive producer, Susanne Boyce, the one who had taken a big chance on me, that she could hire me but that if I bombed it would be on her head. That interview was quoted by the prime minister and netted me a Gemini TV nomination in the same year that I hosted the Gemini Awards themselves, alongside the fabulous Cynthia Dale. I was flying high professionally, but I didn't appreciate the moment in ways that made me in any way wiser.

With *Midday* I learned the art of TV broadcasting. Just like great acting and stand-up, it was about being present, being able to chance being truly curious and most of all being authentic.

Years later when Paul McLaughlin, who had been one of my Ryerson professors, ran advanced training courses for CBC on-air hosts, he would invite me to speak to them for half a day. Here is what I shared:

The bad news is that it's not healthy to want thousands, if not millions, of strangers to love you. The good news is that you actually have the skill and tools to make that happen.

So, now that you have their attention what is it you want to say?

You see, that's really it, at least for me. I knew lots of people in broadcasting, stand-up and acting that were quite content to stop at getting the love. I felt that the love should come from family and the much more difficult journey toward loving myself. The phrase "love of self" has always been problematic for me. It's like the word "ego." Both have come to mean an exaggerated sense of worth, but there are other meanings. Ego, for me, is really about choices. What makes me do or avoid doing something when out in the world? What if I come from a place of insecurity? I must become bigger and command attention like some frightened pufferfish.

One way to achieve some level of security, if not fame, was marquee status. In a country as demographically small as Canada, name recognition for public figures is almost non-existent. Actors with long and illustrious careers go unnoticed and unknown. Does it matter? Hell yes. Without marquee value you have no leverage to command a decent wage for your talents. Besides, you are wanting to be noticed. I used to ensure that my name was included in the title of every show I hosted. After all, this is Canadian showbiz, the witness protection program of public life. In later years I found myself wanting to step away from the spotlight. My ego-chasing days had caused me more pain than joy. Was this retreat about reaching an epiphany, finding wisdom or the satisfaction of arrival? No. It was, for me, a fall from grace.

Friday Night with Ralph Benmergui

I remember walking through the canyon of mid-sized sky-scrapers in uptown Toronto on a blustery winter night. Look-ing up, I literally thought, "One day I'll own this town." This was another in a series of overcompensating moments that had started with that chubby boy pushing leaves down the street, practising his Academy Award acceptance speech. Yeah, I was on my way up. Mind you, I'd had that thought after an unpaid set at Yuk Yuk's and a stolen chicken salad sandwich from the club's kitchen. Nonetheless, fame would be mine.

Midday was going well, I was hosting the Geminis – what could go wrong? The Gemini telecast was watched that year by what was considered a large audience for English-speaking Canada. The biggest for that or any other Gemini telecast, if memory serves. About a million people tuned in, and with some great producing by the likes of head writer Joe Bodolai, and a great production team, the night went off without a hitch. I do remember standing backstage in my tux and thinking, What the hell am I doing? If I bomb out there, it'll be in front of the entire television industry in this country. This was like hitting the stage on a Saturday night at Yuk Yuk's times one hundred. I had just been working on a late-night one-on-one pilot for a talk show with one of the country's best independent producers, but the pilot had not gone well. That night, at the Geminis, nothing could go wrong. I was seated with my wife, and newly minted movie star and SNL favourite Mike Myers. His *Wayne's World* flick had just crossed the hundred-million-dollar mark. He was classically Canadian – authentic and kind to those around him, with a large dollop of shyness and, underneath that, a steel-eyed sense of what funny is all about. My fortunes were changing.

By the next day my phone was ringing. Lawyer/agent Michael Levine was on the line to anoint me into an exclusive club of movers and shakers in the smallish solar system that was and is Canadian stardom. I could write my own ticket. Kind of. Well, not really, but hey who knew? I met with the heads of programming for both major networks. CTV said, "Ralph we love you, but we can't support a late-night TV talk show. Numbers just aren't there." CBC, well they were more intrigued.

I told Ivan Fecan, the then-head of programming at CBC, that I wanted to basically do *The Ed Sullivan Show* with all Canadian talent. I thought that the public broadcaster should be unabashedly enthusiastic about the enormous amount of talent we had, and that a showcase with me on the side in a nice tux would fit the bill. "Lose the tux and we're in business,"

Ivan said. But here's where things got Faustian. I was told that we could get the green light but that the "we" had to change. Instead of the producer I had been working with, who I had piloted the original idea with, I would need a new production team. Perhaps the same team that had just hit a home run with the Geminis would fit the bill. Oh, and by the way, I had to be the one to cut ties with the original producer. I always regret that I didn't have the confidence to say that I liked working with him, that if they wanted to fire him to go right ahead. I didn't have the backbone to do it, though. I cut ties with the producer and we never worked together again. When someone says they have no regrets, don't believe them. I have plenty and that has always been one of them.

I carried on. By now the full weight of the CBC was behind me. We had just moved into the brand-new Broadcast Centre at the foot of Front Street, across from what was then the Skydome, where the Blue Jays were busy winning back-to-back World Series championships. Great, right? But I was getting this awful feeling that I could have whatever I wanted and that everyone wanted to be my friend. Neither struck me as a good place to be in life, work or family, but it was too late to turn back now.

This was going to be a big show – talk, music, comedy, variety. All of it, and all kinds of agendas were at play. Some were obvious, some more insidious.

I remember the late, great showbiz interviewer Brian Linehan coming to see one of the rehearsals and turning to variety head George Anthony, who he had been close to for so many years, and saying, "My God, you've put the entire CBC building on Ralph's back!" Or words very much to that effect. The head of variety wanted a kind of frankly more old-fashioned guest list, and the head of television was shifting the whole evening schedule around and was looking to us to deliver a million eyeballs every Friday. Me, I was trying to walk around like the quarterback everyone was hoping I would be.

We had all the resources you could ask for. The show was going to look like a million bucks, even though it cost a tenth of that per episode. I was now surrounded by people who had the scent of power in their nostrils; I was becoming very much a commodity. Meanwhile, I was getting less and less of myself. I used that experience years later when interviewing John Travolta. I had three minutes to speak with him on a film junket while he was promoting a dreadful movie called *The General's Daughter*. Here's what I asked:

What's it like to fly in to Vancouver?

(He's a pilot and had done two films in Vancouver recently.)

Why do you barnstorm Kirstie Alley's house?

(They were neighbours, and he loved doing that.)

What is an "Assist"?

(He and Alley are Scientologists, and an Assist is a sort of laying-on-of-hands healing that they do.)

With the film company publicist signalling me to wrap it up, I asked one more question:

What effect has having millions of dollars had on your ability to form friendships?

At this last question he bolted upright in his chair. "That is the best question I have had to date," he said. Travolta then went on for a few minutes about finding out who your real friends are and the sad truth that power attracts many, and that falling off that pedestal has the salutary effect of shedding the hangers-on. Without my own fall from grace I would not have asked that question. Travolta had been a superstar, fallen out of favour and was only brought back by the success of Quentin Tarantino's box-office hit *Pulp Fiction*.

Friday Night would teach me a lot. We had a hugely hyped premiere. Don Cherry, the hockey macho man, and Scott Thompson, the flamingly gay member of *The Kids in the Hall*, ended up on a couch beside each other with Scott snuggling up to Don. It was supposed to be Canadiana for the new generation. A million people watched and the executives were ecstatic. One minor note though. The show debuted, at my urging, an hour earlier than what was to become its regular time slot. You see, the latest edition of the flagship news show, *The National*, was making an unfortunate major move, broadcasting an hour earlier at 9:00 p.m. Anchor Peter Mansbridge was going to be joined by Pamela Wallin, who had been poached from rival CTV. It was a big night for appointment television.

The next week we debuted at 10:00 p.m., and the audience was cut in half. Part of it was me, part of it was something much deeper that I didn't understand at the time and would only later become clear. The show was high status, glitzy, slick and screamed Toronto – the one city in Canada that unified all other Canadians in contempt. What we like, as Canadians, and I say this with a good measure of admiration, is low-status public displays. We are averse to hype and bluster. Think about it: the show that I had replaced, *The Tommy Hunter Show*, was the darling of white Christian Canada. "Good night and may God bless." The show that they replaced me with when I was eventually and mercifully cancelled starred the Celtic darling of small-town Canada, Rita MacNeil. I was just some guy with a weird name, visibly uncomfortable and claiming to speak for mainstream Canadian culture. Probably not such a good idea. But forget all that – I wanted to showcase our country's talent, which was largely ignored at home and deserving of a national audience and the full weight of great production values.

We had everybody. The record companies spared no expense in getting us the likes of Céline Dion, Leonard Cohen with his LA backup singers and even the reunion – sans Robbie Robertson – of the Band. It was a thrill to just stand there and say to the camera, "Ladies and gentlemen, Buffy Sainte-Marie." We had Bachman–Turner Overdrive open the show with our house band, bringing the house down with their hit, "Takin' Care of Business." The Rheostatics with Martin Tielli and Hugh Marsh on his electric violin just killed me with their version of Joni Mitchell's "River." When it comes to the showbiz side of me, I am actually pretty corny. I even had the original plate spinner from *The Ed Sullivan Show* on when I found out he was Canadian. I wore original Canadian jackets designed by Indigenous artists. On the night, in the moment, everyone thought the show was electric. At home on TV, for some reason that none of us could really figure out, it wasn't working.

We had Sarah McLachlan debuting her first smash hit, the Barenaked Ladies doing two songs on our first show from their breakout album, *Gordon*. Bruce Cockburn, Junkhouse, the Pursuit of Happiness. We had all the comics I had started out with doing stand-up on a national stage. When Brian Mulroney resigned, I opened the show with a picture of him framed by a funeral wreath dressed as a preacher. I delivered a eulogy and then burst into song. It was one the writers had come up with, called "He's Gone!" The curtain rose behind me and a full gospel choir belted it out as I walked into an audience clapping fiercely along.

I had gone from interviewing very serious people about the state of national and global affairs to funnyman host of a variety show. But my opening monologues were too stiff. I had lost the spontaneity in my interviewing with all the prep and tech run-through. Peter Mansbridge kindly took me out to lunch to remind me that interviewing was what I did best, and to throw way the cue cards and just relax. But I felt out of my skin. Detached from my actual life – the one where I walked the dog and wanted to be home.

We soldiered on as the ratings slowly descended into dangerous territory. The critics hated us. To be precise, they hated me. There was blood in the water. I would wring my hands during the monologue. Wince when the bandleader had the crowd chant my name. Frankly, I wasn't able to throw myself wholeheartedly into the showbiz-or-bust tank. I had just come from the current affairs world, and deep down I knew that was much more me. I even had the thought that it wasn't right to do the show on the Jewish Sabbath.

On my previous show, *Midday*, I had been wondering what to do with my desire to deepen my relationship with Judaism. I began to ask myself questions like: What if I just showed up on set one day wearing a kippah? I had returned to Judaism in my late twenties in a way that many do. I had wandered off earlier and spent time exploring all the facets that made up the diamond of my spiritual life. But I had come back for the tradition and the family glue that oozes out once children arrive. I attended synagogue again and was immersed in Jewish thought and innovation.

So what, I would muse as I drove to work each day, if I just arrived with the obvious sign of my religion, my kippah, atop my head? What would the current affairs honchos do? Would I be asked to remove it before going on air? If so, why? Would it be assumed that if I were interviewing someone about the Gulf War, for instance, that I would be proclaiming a bias toward the interests of Israel? For years now people have assumed that to be Jewish is to be pro-Israeli policy, to not be able to think critically about the region and to be an automatic Zionist. Then should they not also have assumed that I would be anti-communist after a lifetime of being fed stories of atrocity and deprivation? That I would cleave unquestioningly to the dusty tropes of the "free world" and the miracle of the free markets? For that matter, how could I interview someone with a neo-conservative ideology if, in my own way of thinking, that ideology led to growing poverty and obscene concentrations of wealth?

The answer to me was obvious. The secret sauce of journalism was and is genuine curiosity. Critical and well-researched thinking must inform every interview, and societal assumptions must be seen as just that: assumptions. Disruptive, yes, but I have always been that way. Indeed, once I had arrived at the network-level of current affairs, the invitations to the circle of what was later termed white privilege arrived at my desk. To be in the mid-to-upper levels of media was to be part of the power. What I found disturbing was the ease with which so many of us elbowed our way to the dessert table, and the nod and wink of those that we had been tasked to hold accountable.

So, what if I wore a kippah? Would I be asked to stay off the air, reassigned in some balletic HR move that would avoid the charge of discrimination? Do we assume that organized religion carries deep bias but that secularism is more non-committal? Is the atheist any less orthodox than the religious person who believes in Christ the Saviour?

I never tested these limits. I was doing well and I had a family to feed. I guess the feeling stayed with me as I hit the spotlight on what was later referred to as "The ill-fated *Friday Night* with Ralph Benmergui." I soldiered on, wondering, What am I doing here with all these people staring at me? An uncomfortable feeling grew in the pit of my stomach: this was not my calling. I had climbed the skyscrapers of Canadian notoriety, just as planned, and found the view from atop sorely lacking.

I had more than my share of scorn tossed my way during the run of *Friday Night*. Some I deserved, some was viscerally dark and uncalled for. Like I said, it's a blood-in-the-water sport, and I was the one bleeding. I remember riding my bike home from the towering new CBC building and seeing the cover of *Frank*, a satirical magazine that revelled in taking the piss out of those that would claim centre stage in politics, media or occasionally the arts. I don't remember what they were saying but it was a basket of insults and humiliations directed squarely at me. I cycled on, and once home I sat with my two young boys. They had no idea what a maelstrom had formed around me. I found great comfort in that. I knew that who I was attempting to become, as a person, was not to be confused with what I did for a living.

I did grow lonely, though. I lost my way, fearful and craving affirmation wherever I could get it. My life was filled with hangers-on. I didn't realize it the day I was called into the network executive's office to be told that the show was cancelled, but I had been given a blessing. I began my fall from grace.

Jump! You'll Grow Wings on the Way Down

With the show cancelled I travelled with my family to Costa Rica for a month. I was exhausted. The waves came crashing in close to our yurt-like cabin at the vegetarian resort we had booked. I worried about what I, the sole provider at the time, would do. Who would hire me? In the States it seemed that if something didn't work at the higher levels of the entertainment business, they just cooked up some other way to capitalize on the fact that you had marquee value. Back home it always seems like we figure that so-and-so had their chance now let someone else give it a go, after all there are only so many seats on the good ship Canada.

I slept, I schemed. I watched bootlegged Disney laserdiscs

at the restaurant with local kids gathered round. I practised my Spanish – not much call for that in Canada.

I returned in time for the Gemini Awards and was presenting with my old co-host, Valerie Pringle. She introduced me as "What's left of my friend Ralph." I walked onstage bearded and tanned but not relaxed. I received some mild if not pitying applause. Then Seaton McLean, co-founder of Atlantis Films, one of the country's most successful production companies, stood up as if to say, "Good on ya, Ralph, you gave it a real go." I will always remember that simple act of kindness.

I spent the next eight months writing a never-to-be-published book and meditating every day. I immersed myself in the Buddha's dharma; read *The Tibetan Book of Living and Dying*, by Sogyal Rinpoche, and then *Seeking the Heart of Wisdom*, by American writers Jack Kornfield and Joseph Goldstein. They are part of what is affectionately known as the JuBu Movement. Many of the leaders of the North American Buddhist movement are Jews. I am still a borderline JuBu in many ways. The stillness and presence that are core to the meditative practice were, and still are, good medicine for my aching spirit.

Taking what I learned about my country through *Friday Night* – that we are humble people who enjoy modest entertainment – I began to turn away from the showbiz beast. If you want to be big, go to LA or New York. We'll love you and claim you as our own if you make it in either of those arenas, but if you're staying, keep it simple. I don't think that's a bad thing, it's just a thing I learned. The rest of my career has been more in line with that truth.

I had a lot of repair work to do. My marriage had taken a beating and I had used up much of my professional capital.

One day I noticed that the head of the CRTC (Canadian Radio-television and Telecommunications Commission), Keith Spicer, had been swirling around the country, cape and hat in hand, proclaiming the inadequacies of the CBC. He did so without mentioning that each year the budget had been slashed, that the political masters of both Liberal and Conservative stripe had starved the public broadcaster and forced it to seek profit and pop appeal, implementing a year-by-year budgetary stranglehold around the throat of the corporation.

I wrote an op-ed in rebuttal, and Jim Byrd, a lovely man from Newfoundland who was now running the TV side of the CBC, got in touch. He asked if I would go to lunch with him. I arrived on my bike, we sat and talked, and he asked if I would like to work at NewsWorld. I said sure, but really I was so grateful that I wanted to hug him right there in the restaurant.

It was good to know that someone believed in me. It was better to know that I could still make a living despite the media stoning I had just been through. I spent the next six years hosting a small town hall–style show in the atrium of the CBC building in Toronto: *Benmergui Live*. We scraped by barely noticed but we also had a lot of fun. The pressure was off.

I used to have a bet with the show's director, Michele Berlyne. We would bet to see how long it would take for someone to get on the line and open with, "Hi, Ben." It happened almost every day. Soon as I heard it, I would look straight into the camera and slowly widen my eyes. I would hear Michele laughing in my earpiece whenever I did this. She had been my director on *Midday* and I loved working with her. Also on staff was someone I had first met when I did a few months of call-in on the Ontario-region *Radio Noon* show. Jennifer Dettman had been a part-time chase producer booking guests and generating show ideas. They wanted to cut her for budgetary purposes, but I said they were nuts. She stayed and came with me to *Benmergui Live*. She left later to produce Strombo's national talk show and went on to become a senior part of the CBC TV seventh floor group. Jennifer Dettman was truly the best chase producer and idea generator I ever had the pleasure of working with.

We were live the day the O.J. Simpson trial released its verdict. You could have heard a pin drop across North America that day. O.J. had already revolutionized all news television with his slow-motion Ford Bronco escape through LA. That event alone had literally birthed the now completely meaningless phrase "Breaking News."

The verdict was read live. Not guilty. I couldn't believe it. We were flooded with calls. I have always loved live broadcasting – it keeps you in the present. If I had my way, we would have played Don McLean's "American Pie" at that moment.

We also did a live show from the Warkworth Institution in Ontario, where we assembled a gymnasium filled with men who had been sentenced to life in prison. It's important to know a few things here. First off, they were all there voluntarily. Jennifer and I had driven up to see them in a classroom at the prison, to talk to them and to gain their trust that we were there to hear their truth as people and not just convicts. Believe me, some of them had done horrible things – murder, sexual predation. There was even a professional hit man who wiled away his time on the range popping pills and playing pool. But the thing is, a life sentence is a misnomer. These men were really going to be there for anywhere from eight to possibly seventeen years depending on how they behaved and what programs they completed while penned up.

The question we asked the national audience that night was: What should we do with these men? Some said throw away the key. Some said rehabilitate. Most didn't realize that one day they would be sitting beside one of these men at their local coffee shop. It was tough to go into that prison every day as we prepared for the show while learning more, like the fact that murderers are the least likely to reoffend. That in many cases, hit man excluded, these were acts of passion or psychotic breaks. Every day we would leave, one gate would open and then close behind us, then another gate would open and close behind us. As I looked back, I thought it so strange that these men would spend years never going out to get groceries, catch a local hockey game, be free. They had forfeited that right. One thing I did know was that prison could easily harden your heart, break your spirit and spit you out onto the street doomed for failure. An eye for an eye was not meant to justify savage jailings; it was meant to ensure that compensation for foul deeds obligated the perpetrator to make things right. We did some great shows on that small program. I liked hearing from people every day and I was grateful to still be on the air.

But *Friday Night* had bruised me more than I realized. Occasionally I would try to land a bigger fish as I toiled away in the atrium. In fact, there came a time when I was up for a major network radio show that would run from nine till noon on weekdays. The *Morningside* of its time. I wanted that show very much. I never felt as comfortable on TV as I did on radio. It was a more intimate medium, and frankly more soulful.

I was walking home the day they informed me that I didn't get it. I stopped to take the call, and when they said goodbye I turned into a small alleyway and, for one of the few times in my broadcast life, I cried. I felt I had been born to do that job. From then on, I knew my days at the CBC were numbered. My life was changing, my marriage was crumbling, that chapter of my life was coming to an end. I didn't plan any of this, it just came together – and apart, as it were. Without realizing it I was entering the autumn of my life. I wasn't there yet but the crimson trees were there, just over the horizon.

It was time to leave the CBC. Luckily, I was asked to join my old producer from my Winnipeg days, Ross Porter, at Jazz. FM91. He was the new CEO and I managed to end up as the morning show host. Ross was creating a small miracle, a 24-7 all-jazz, real jazz station in Canada's biggest media market. The place was abuzz, and it was an up-and-down ride over the next six years. During that time I got remarried and had another two children. I was also finally free to get involved in politics – oh, and I had a lot more grey in my beard.

Who's Ralph Benmergui?
Get Me Ralph Benmergui.
Get Me a Young Ralph Benmergui.
Who's Ralph Benmergui?

Part of the work of becoming an elder is crossing the bridge from ego to eco. How can I become part of the greater landscape of community? How can I become useful as a mentor? Noble thoughts to be sure. But if we add in the prevailing attitudes toward us as we age into elderhood, the task becomes freighted with systemic bias against the very idea of age. We wonder if we will even be asked to contribute. The notion of retirement itself implies a torpor where we linger over morning coffees till near noon. We're expected to watch all-news TV channels, populated as they are with commercials for stairlifts, adult diapers and pharmaceuticals with a list of side effects that usually concludes by informing you that in some cases this medication may cause death. Instead of connecting we are supposed to sit quietly, hoping that perhaps we'll be hearing from someone we have known or, if we're lucky, loved. Retirement seems so much like surrender at first glance. Even an active retirement is for many a segregated experience. More and more of us would rather cling to the last workaday version of ourselves than venture into the isolating future of having no work. But what could we do to make our leave-taking from full-time work meaningful?

One thing that we have pruned from the tree of life experience in our rush to secularism is the ability to celebrate the rites of passage with meaningful and sacred rituals. To even hint at how holy our brief time together is can be difficult for many of us. Too intimate. I was once leading a workshop, a men's group on Age-ing to Sage-ing. Halfway through the first session, one of the men, a bear of a man, said, "Is this going to be one of those airy-fairy things?" I found myself wanting to reassure him but decided against it. "Yes," I said as I looked him in the eye. "Yes, it is." He turned out to be a valuable member of the group and we shared many tender moments together as he spoke of his love of family, and his desire to find a new way of seeing himself and the place of work in his life as he approached seventy.

So, let's get airy-fairy. Imagine, instead of simply being shown the door, what a leaving ritual might look like. Picture those that you have worked closely with gathered in a circle, facing one another in a shared space without power structures.

We all bring an artifact, something that reminds us of the person leaving and what they have meant to us – a picture, a project file, a shared road trip symbolized by a rent-a-car key fob. We place these artifacts on a table in the centre of the circle and tell the stories behind them. A facilitator speaks of the power that work and time together can mean. About the fact that this has not just been passing time but a witnessing of each other as we move though this life. The person leaving can speak of what it has meant to be a part of this circle, what they wish for those around them, and then each co-worker bestows a wish or blessing on the person exiting the work environment.

Martin Buber talks of the difference between an "I–It" relationship where we see the other in an objectified way, only considering what use a person can be and engaging with them in a transactional space filled with notions of deficit and surplus, and an "I–Thou" relationship where we connect with mutuality, directness, presentness, intensity and ineffability. I think of this as connecting on the plane of soul, heart to heart. Spirituality is about relationship – to ourselves, to each other and to the deep mystery of the unknown. It is an acknowledgement that there is a divinely unknowable spark within everything, and that our soulful work is not to find it in others as much as to allow the hardened shell, the klipah as we say in Judaism, to soften and fall away, allowing our deeper meaning and true self to emerge so that others can see it.

It is said that God can only enter through a broken heart. If I believe God to be a process and not a thing then that idea takes a different shape. It looks more like humility and an opening to what is, right now, and never will be again. Humility is not about the humbling we associate with shame and penitence;

humility, I have learned, is knowing what your proper positioning is in any given situation. Would I serve this situation best by following, leading, listening or speaking? Humility is presence tinged with grace.

So as we sit with the person leaving our workplace, why not make it personal? Working with others is personal. It requires courage to make that a conscious piece of our lives and to do more than playfully punch their arm as we shuffle back to our desks, knowing that we won't connect again. Imagine as well that we bring our elders back to share their wisdom as we soldier on in our own endeavours. Even the concept of generations has changed as we carve out market segments to sell to. It used to be that a generation was a forty-year span; now it's less than twenty years before the next wave must crash against the beachheads, the better to flood the halls of our shopping malls.

Leaving for another position with the feeling that there are still years of work ahead of you is one way to exit. But I have realized that the story changes when you are leaving a career or an organization while in your sixties. We live longer now than anyone has in human history. It's not uncommon for a "retiree" to have another twenty years of living left. Mary Jordan and Kevin Sullivan wrote in a 2017 article for the *Washington Post* that people are living longer, more expensive lives, often without much of a safety net. As a result, record numbers of Americans older than sixty-five are working – now nearly one in five. That proportion has risen steadily over the past decade, and at a far faster rate than for any other age group. Today, nine million senior citizens work, compared to four million in 2000.

In speaking to people over fifty who have, for one reason or another, had to find new employment, opportunities can become harder to find than they imagined. At first, they simply assume that with a powerful resumé and lots of gas still in the tank they will be scooped up by another employer. I certainly assumed that when I was relieved of my duties at one of my later positions.

In a late-afternoon meeting with the president of Sheridan College, he informed me that I was enjoying my last day there and handed me a manila envelope that contained a severance offer. "You don't need to look it over now," he said. I was stunned. As I left, my mind swirling, wondering what I was going to say to my beloved wife, I muttered, "Thank you for the opportunity." I went to my office to grab a few essentials, having been told that I could pick up the rest on the weekend. From inside my office I heard work colleagues going about their day, one wondering if anyone had seen "the Rabbi," as she lovingly called me. I did not respond. What I didn't realize that day was that I was now a man reaching sixty. That people looking for someone to invest in saw little runway in someone like me, even if the resumé was, as many had said, very good.

My heart sank as it does for most people when they, like Nachshon in the bible, are pushed into the raging sea of uncertainty. I may be older, but at that time I still had two of my four children at home, both school aged. Retirement and a condo downsize were not in the cards. Of course, there would be no closing ritual with heartfelt stories to share with colleagues. I had poured my heart into the work, as so many do. No, I was simply asked to take a few things, come back after hours to get the rest and leave like a thief in the night. It would be a year before I returned to that president's office to meet with his successor, a valued friend. I told her that it was hard for me to be there. That I had basically vanished as far as anyone there was concerned. I probably made her uncomfortable in mentioning it, but I have come to believe that what is left under the surface festers, leaving the tart taste of regret or even bitterness on my tongue. When that meeting ended, I walked the familiar rabbit warren of offices and support staff carols. People came out, gave me a hug, asked how I had been and said that they had missed me. That closure meant a lot, but I didn't share with them what happened since my departure.

I soldiered on. Each resumé had to be tailored to each job. Communications, external relations, innovation, post-secondary, media. At age sixty, I thought I had a well-rounded CV. But something strange happened. I wasn't getting the response I was used to. People were being kind, but they were passing. One headhunter called to tell me that she had pushed hard to have me seen for the final round of interviews but that she was sorry to say they were going in a different direction. The successful candidate was very well qualified – and twenty-five years younger. For some jobs I didn't even receive a courtesy interview, and these were jobs that I was confident I could do at the highest level of competence. I looked at the pitch document for the public broadcaster, my one-time employer of some twenty-one years – programming must be young and diverse.

In Hindu culture, there are four stages of life. Those in their thirties and forties are in "Grihastha," the second stage, as householders, acquiring goods, providing hearth and home for their growing families. The ego is in harnessing and producing tangible benefits. I have always referred to it as keeping the fridge full. But by the time we arrive at the fork in the road, the place where we journey into elderhood, we yearn to walk into the forest and sit quietly as we reflect on a life's worth of effort. This retreat and deepening of spiritual practice, Vanaprastha, is the third stage. The change in life expectancy obviously bring new challenges to the aging table. How do we finance twenty more years of life in a culture that values youth in everything, especially the workplace? Younger employees, still in the acquisitive stage of their lives, might work more hours, have less family to pull them away from the desk and often demand less money than older employees who rightfully expect to be compensated for their accumulated experience and, yes, wisdom.

The fastest-growing cohort of entrepreneurs in North America are people like me, those fifty-five or older who have had to go out and become their own boss. In many cases not because they want to but because they find that employers and decision makers are looking over their shoulders like some distracted career climber at a cocktail party searching for the next young star.

The challenge should not be how we become better entrepreneurs. I believe that the shift to entrepreneurism that I witnessed in colleges and universities, as well as in the tech hubs of Silicon Valley and other urban superclusters, is a false narrative. Very few people are suited to entrepreneurship, with its spectacular failure rates, high risk and long-term investment structures, not to mention the drive and deep resilience required to succeed. What the romantic storyline of the genius/rebel covers up is that work itself has died in its twentieth-century form. The gold watch and mutual loyalties of employer and employee have vanished, and we are left instead with a work culture filled with precarity. Occasional contract opportunities have become the norm. No group health plans, no pension contributions from employers and no sense of community and continuity that comes with long-term investment in each other and our gifts.

How do we age into that environment? Where do we place our hearts in that "sometime" workplace? This is not simply a question for those approaching the autumn of their work lives, but there is one piece that applies mostly to that group. If there is no "there" there, where do we deposit our hard-earned wisdom? And who can benefit from it?

When I first began at the CBC, there were departments for arts programming and for current affairs, as opposed to news gathering. We had producers employed on a full-time basis to come up with truly Canadian programming that reflected the best principles of public-over-private broadcasting. But successive governments of different political stripes have continued to tether the public broadcaster year by year by underfunding it. As one senior executive admitted at a dinner I attended, "We are going to use private broadcasting methods to save the public broadcaster."

My fellow dinner guests didn't bat an eye, but in my opinion, this was a disastrous decision from which the CBC, in particular the television side, has never recovered. Those full-time productive culture workers were shown the door, departments died, contracts became shorter and shorter. We lost what continuity gives to storytelling. We lost our wisdom. Over the years, CBC radio has done much with little; TV on the other hand is in desperate need of a total makeover. Though the regional information shows have not changed formats in forty years, there is still more ability for them to pivot and change with the times. On the other hand, blowing up CBC TV and making it a content generator for dissemination to all Canadians without market-driven imperatives means a smaller presence unfiltered and in touch with the evolving Canadian story.

Old and Improved

In our rush to join the marketing stampede that slices and dices us according to age and income, we have lost something of the public good. That's been a big piece for me, that loosening of community bonds. I grew up in an extended family, with multiple cousins, aunts and uncles that had a firm grip on my little kid cheeks as they pinched my flesh and called me Raffi. They hugged and scolded me like I was one of their own. Now we live alone, asking too much of our nuclear families and chasing so much that matters so little. Those days are gone, and now my fear is that not only do we live alone but far worse, we are scared that in the end we will die alone as well.

There are now a billion people on planet Earth over the age of sixty, and that population is growing fast. Yet no marketing person in their right mind would sell you a product that is "old and improved." But what if it's true? Lewis Richmond wrote in an article titled "The Dharma of Aging" that "research on aging (and there are lots of it now) has discovered many aspects of our life that actually improve with age. One of them is 'integrative problem solving.' Yes, we may be slower at math problems or word retrieval, but we are better at putting together a creative solution to a complex problem that requires a lot of life experience, as well as a lot of practice in solving such problems. Older people do measurably better at such tasks than younger people do." Integrative problem solving, precisely the skill set that makes wisdom such a valuable and relevant tool in our innovation culture. One that we are told is the domain of the young, hip and mobile.

Presently we are mired in an old paradigm of evaluation. Job descriptions today have become grotesque parodies of what any reasonable employer should expect from an employee. "We are looking for a highly motivated energetic individual who is willing to give everything they've got. Must be proficient in Word, Adobe, Excel. Able to navigate and populate all social media platforms, proficient in (insert absurd list of skills here.)"

It has become normal for the least amount of people to do the most amount of work. In my hiring experience in large organizations, the human resources lead in an interview most often ends by asking, "Are you willing to work occasional evenings and weekends?" As you can imagine, the reply is usually a reluctant "yes" delivered through a tight smiling mask of enthusiasm. With an older applicant, I would offer that there is often an unconscious bias that is layered on top of all these chocolate-coated, take-one-for-the-Gipper demands. That is, the assumption that older people are not interested in staying till ten at night.

Or going out for drinks after work for that matter. We are in a different geography of our lives. Remember the Hindu view of life stages. In our elderhood we become more contemplative. Stillness accompanies us as our bodies yearn for respite. Our minds turn toward the bigger questions of life. I am left wondering if I can harvest and cultivate all that I have seen, felt, heard.

Could it be that we can ask for something different than simply throwing ourselves into the fire of some other person's dreams? Make no mistake, the young may have the energy and lack of commitments to family and community that elders carry, but they too feel the soul-sucking emptiness that throws life out of balance.

Imagine a different job description. Imagine instead a call, not for kamikaze foot soldiers but for someone who can serve as a motivated team member, committed and connected, at any age.

"If you're interested in living a balanced life and making a healthy and well-respected contribution to an exciting company, we should talk. We accept the fact that you have friends and family, and that your work life and your community should complement and not cancel each other. Certain skill sets are required, and if there are any gaps in your knowledge of operating systems or if you want to upgrade certain skills to help make us a better organization we will assist in identifying opportunities that you can take advantage of with the understanding that we have requirements, deadlines and responsibilities to our customers, all of which are baseline requirements for employment.

"Apply here."

*

My journey into precarious work dovetails with a sea change in work culture that is affecting all generations. The difference for me is that I am not looked upon as brimming with potential. Wisdom is not asked for – or apparently needed – in today's work environment. In fact, it could well be seen as old thinking. Ageism is real. I don't think it's conscious, but I take no chances. I shave off my beard if I have a job interview – a grey beard is only hip if you own the company, and I don't.

The effect of all this precarity has been deeply upsetting for me. It has challenged the version of myself that I've been busily constructing all these years. I hadn't realized how easily I had moved into a place of entitlement. It wasn't about if, it was about when. Yes, I had worked hard, remained nimble and taken chances that others wouldn't have, but looking back I don't remember when I crossed the line. You know the one. It's one we use in show business quite a bit.

Who's Ralph Benmergui?

Get me Ralph Benmergui.

Get me a young Ralph Benmergui.

Who's Ralph Benmergui?

Yet, something else is going on. Something liberating. As some might say, I have come to the proverbial fork in the road and have decided that the way forward is about moving from success to significance. This is not an easy turn to make, and despite myself I have been wrestling with the choice for these last few years. Only recently have I carved out a space for this idea to inform my intention, my kavanah as we say in Hebrew. The first glimmers actually appeared when I was young, those moments in my early twenties when I dared to dream, when I yearned to change the world. But as providing and consuming took hold of me, I pivoted and surrendered the fight. I opted instead for success and a mild case of materialism. The material can become the measure of a person: It's not just a car or house, it's *the* car, *the* house. In fairness I have not been that guy. I have always frankly seen that pursuit as comical at best. Ownership for me is delusional. Everything, and I do mean everything, is a rental.

So, how do we take that turn into autumn? Now is the time to harvest my wisdom and share it as best I can. This has become what's important to me, the legacy that I wish to leave, which will guide my choices and become the measure of my new vision of success. What drives us all is purpose, according to Viktor Frankl, Holocaust survivor and author of the classic book *Man's Search for Meaning*. Work can give us exterior objectives and, if we're lucky enough, a healthy dollop of purpose, but I do believe that if we are to decouple from the exterior affirmation that work and career can give us, we must look inward. When many are on their deathbeds, they speak not of the things they did or had but of the love they treasure. When people die and are resuscitated, regardless of cultural predisposition, they often speak of a pure love that enveloped them, devoid of judgment. If we cultivate the still-small voice within us, it will reveal the deeper yearnings of our lives. We can find a drive that is fuelled not by accomplishment but by the most essential element, love.

I have come to believe that if this informs our sense of purpose then we can reinvigorate work and home life in a way that we yearn for. We can bring all of ourselves to our labours, and bring our labours into harmony with the living world we have been gifted with.

Working precariously has given me, for one of the few times in my working life, a glimpse at what it means to watch the parade pass by instead of running to be at the front of it. My initial reaction was one of panic and no small measure of guilt. The feeling that I was letting loved ones down. But a more fertile ground has also been created. If I can slow my breath and make myself available to the opportunity, I can catch glimpses of something new. A sense of grace, and with it the calm that lets me think and act from a slightly different place. A site of soulfulness that takes its cues from the heart as much as the head. I am not giving up, but perhaps as the southern Rabbi I quoted earlier says, I am shifting from success to significance, trusting that I will not disappear but will instead emerge with clear eyes and a gentler hand on the tiller of work.

As one fellow traveller put it, "I am sixty-one and coming to terms with aging, that is to say gracefully and not with disappointment. I have reached many goals, which no longer inspire. Yet I am aware that life is precious. This feels like a different stage, as tough as adolescence was."

What a wonderful insight. Moving into her sixties, this accomplished woman now longs to be graceful, not resentful. I have never thought to put adolescence and elderhood in the same sentence, but maybe we should. They are both passages into unknown territory and accompanied by often dramatic physical changes. Both challenge us to see ourselves in unfamiliar ways. To find new ways to self-identify.

From householder to forest dweller, we can work and we do for a very long time. What we bring to the enterprise can be guided by a different compass that accepts mortality and is informed by wisdom and generosity.

Politics, Jazz and *Friday Night 2.0*

After twenty years at CBC, it was time to spread my political wings. It had been liberating and constricting at the same time to remain agnostic in the political arena. I remember once, on the trip I took to London, England, I went out onto the street during a rare morning off and saw a huge crowd marching toward Hyde Park for a Free Nelson Mandela concert. The crowd was filled with energy and righteous indignation. I followed, but out of pure conditioning I stayed on the sidewalk. I would not join them. As a public broadcaster it wasn't my place. But now all of that was behind me and I could engage in politics. I still hosted a radio show but it was a jazz program and I didn't discuss politics on the air.

My first foray was with the political party I had grown up with, the NDP. As a kid we lived in the federal riding held at that time by the Jewish leader of the NDP, David Lewis. My father was a union man, the shop steward for CUPE Local 79 Toronto, inside city workers. I have always believed strongly in unions and the security and protections they fight for every day. One cold day in a downtown coffee shop I spoke with the late Jack Layton and his political and spiritual soulmate, Olivia Chow, about possibly working together. Perhaps I could be part of his communications team, perhaps I could even run. I remembered a day years earlier, when I was away on business, pacing around my hotel room, thinking that I would spend ten years in showbiz, ten years in journalism and then ten in politics. Was this going to be that pivot point? Granted I had already spent thirty years in total on the first two goals, but I still had lots of fuel left in the tank. We had a good talk.

To me, Jack had always been a man on a mission. A classic NDP warrior. The "dippers," as they are known in political parlance, fight. For, and with, just about everyone. I think this comes from years spent in opposition in many parts of the country and at the federal level. This approach has pluses and minuses, but I believed that they were often on the right side of the public conversation. We agreed that what he could offer me as a position would not meet my family's financial needs, so instead we mused about me running for office. An election would be in the offing in the next year or so. He offered the riding where I had grown up, but the truth was that the NDP didn't have a chance in hell of winning it. I took it as an indication that they weren't seeing a future for me in the party. I began to search for a different way to get political.

I don't know how I feel about coincidence, but my next political moment only happened because I was sitting naked in a steam bath at the gym with another man on the other side of the shvitz, as it's known in Yiddish. After all, it was the Jewish Community Centre we were sweating in. I broke the customary silence that is part of shvitz etiquette and said, "Excuse me, I hate to bother you, but you're young: Why do you vote for the NDP?" He said he didn't. I pressed on: "Why? I would think their progressive policies would attract people in your age group." He didn't agree. "Actually," he said through the mist and heat, "I don't vote NDP because I work for the Green Party."

We talked more back in the change room. He was an organizer and helped find candidates and work on campaigns while looking for the first Green seat in Canada. Our conversation ended with him asking if I would like to meet the Green Leader, Elizabeth May. She was coming to Toronto in a few weeks and we could meet near the train station before she departed for headquarters in Ottawa. I was intrigued and said yes. I had interviewed Elizabeth a few times and she would have known me as well in that media way.

I read their platform. I agreed with just about all of it, but most importantly they didn't have the stench of power drawing them into moral and political ambiguity for the sake of winning enough seats to run the show. It meant, I thought, that they could think about what might truly help people and the planet to survive the threat of global and local climate destruction.

The idea that I could make a difference has been a main driver for me for most of my adult life. Even as a child I imagined myself standing on a stage behind great leaders like Martin Luther King, Jr., and Bobby Kennedy, bringing my little Jewish voice to their struggle for those yearning for expression and equality. When both these men were gunned down, I, at twelve years of age, was heartbroken. Once again, the American dream had died. Many small deaths in that country have occurred around race and wealth. It's my belief that America has never accepted the outcome of the Civil War, and that it goes on to this day in a kind of torturous slow motion.

Twined with this yearning for social justice was, and is to this day, a spiritual journey that has me focusing on Torah teachings such as love the stranger as yourself and do not do to another what you would not have them do to you. I have little space in me for the idea that we are just a collection of chemical and synaptic triggers, firing off and then disappearing into the chasm of futility. It might be true, but I'll be damned if that is the compass for my journey in this world. It's just too small a window for me to look out of. I believe in mystery as much as science. In fact, I believe science is our human attempt at articulating the mechanisms responsible for the wonder and awe of creation. A flow that I prefer, for lack of a sufficient word, to call God.

One of the great failings of the progressive movement, of which I count myself a part of, is the separation of spirituality and secular politics. Dr. King and, here in Canada, leaders like Tommy Douglas, a Christian cleric, have breathed life into the call for dignity and equity for the dispossessed above all else. They are right when they say that a society is judged by the way they treat those that have the least power. It is the quality of our mercy that defines us.

I spent the next week or so coming up with what I thought was a way for the Greens to communicate their message of a green and caring society. I organized the policies into three buckets and even put together a PowerPoint. Anyone who knows me knows that slide decks are not my thing. I was pumped.

Elizabeth was charming. She always is. She was also, on first meeting and like many public figures, an odd mix of glass and steel. She had the guts and nerve of a real warrior but also a glass-thin shell that felt as if it might crack in the face of resistance from those around her. I came to realize that loyalty was of the highest value, and that opposition was a violation of that.

She loved my proposal and asked me to become her senior advisor. I was still on the radio at a non-profit station so I had to keep my contribution low key. I liked that, and most of my political contributions, especially to Greens, have been of that nature ever since.

Life was on the exhale for me. I had four children now instead of two. I'd had a first wife, and now I had a second. I was deeply in love and saw new horizons after many years at the CBC.

I would do a morning show every weekday morning and fly to Ottawa once a week for the latter part of the day to work on communications and policy advice.

Mixed into this ferment of creative juices was a series of documentary programs about something I had always wanted to pursue but never got the chance to – spirituality. The first series, produced with my good friend Allan Novak, was called *5 Seekers*. We put out a call for five people who had given up on their birth religion but were still seeking a spiritual direction in life. We received hundreds of applicants. I would say a full third, if not more, came from lapsed Catholics. The rest were Protestant, a very few Jews, and no Muslim or Hindu adherents.

On reflection, I would suggest that those in the dominant culture, Christians, felt more comfortable in disclosing their religious ancestry, and that the rest of us had learned to hide our light under a bushel as a result. I could be wrong. I loved doing that show. We broke the filming into two locations: Sedona, Arizona, and Cortes Island, BC.

We arrived at Sedona as snow was falling. It's situated at an altitude of 1,326 metres. The air is thinner but the scenery is almost literally out of this world. Red rock canyons, wind-sculpted plateaus and stand-alone hoodoos. The ambience is Martian-like, and every ten minutes of trail walking gives you an entirely different vista.

Our seekers were an eccentric lot. One man was blind, crusty and intense, and had a guide dog; another was in his late thirties and had survived HIV; and there was a rural Albertan with a heart of gold. The other two were harder for me to figure out. An attractive and soft-spoken woman who had given up on religion but still seemed to have faith, and finally, a monk-like figure who seemed in many ways unavailable to the experience except as a detached and perhaps superior observer.

Sedona is the New Age capital of America. Didgeridoos, hand drums, bells, crystals, shamanic robes – the town is packed with them. There's even a synagogue thrown in for good measure. The seekers did sound therapy, past life regression and shamanic rituals with a Hopi elder.

I was their guide/television host. I would debrief them after each experience – sometimes they cried, sometimes they winced. It occurred to me that most of them were hoping for a divine bolt of lightning to shock them out of their spiritual bunkers and bring them into the loving light of God, or whatever. I felt sad as I witnessed their yearning. Not that I lean toward certainty when it comes to my spirituality – I don't. It's just that I could feel how much they ached for a deeper meaning, for something strong to cleave to.

We moved on from Sedona to a small island off the coast of British Columbia only accessible by boat. Cortes is home to the Hollyhock retreat centre, which runs alternative programming and leadership programs throughout the year. We had the place to ourselves for the week. It was a very intense time, and the seekers were fraying at the edges. They weren't just filling their spirit-seeking plates at the celestial buffet; they were being recorded all day and well into the night. The more I saw of their god-wrestling the more I was grateful that as flawed as my and all religions are, they at least give structure to the spiritual journey through ritual, text study and community. These things were missing for most of these seekers.

I did two more six-part documentary series. One, called *God Bless America*, was about religion and politics in the run-up to the first Obama presidency. The part from that experience that I still roll around in my head was a dinner that had been set up for me in the suburbs of Virginia with Washington evangelical lobbyist George Roller. They called him "the Holy Roller." We had been visiting with a Black civil rights hero earlier in the day, and the next day we were going to talk to the head of the American Humanist Association. That's a tough gig. The Humanist Association is one of those organizations filled with members who usually resist joining any group at all.

But this night we were in the Virginia suburbs just a stone's throw from DC. George and his wife laid out a spread for us. To be precise, Mrs. Roller did all the cooking. During dinner we talked about their deep love of everyone through the devotion they felt for their Lord and Saviour, Jesus Christ. I pressed them on the idea that their mission in Washington, and on this particular evening with me, was to share the gospel and save my soul. I tried to impress upon George that I found myself offended by his crusade. If I could only find salvation through Jesus, then what did that say about my Jewish belief system? What kind of respect did it show for me and the millions of Jews that came before me? It was a gentle and passion-filled conversation. When asked if they kept pursuing folks, especially those that appeared in some ways lost, Mrs. Roller said in a hushed tone, eyes almost bursting out of their sockets, "If there's low-hanging fruit, we're going to pick it." Then she passed the casserole.

I had always wanted to do a series of documentaries about religion. I wanted us to go below the surface of the religious conversation and explore with genuine curiosity the what and the why of what people believed or didn't.

Say what you want about American culture, it is passionate and dynamic in its breath of practice and opinion. Much more so than we Canadians. It helps to remember that their colonizers were in part religious zealots and social disruptors that came across to Providence and New Amsterdam to throw off the shackles of mainstream religion in England.

In Brooklyn, I met up with Jay Bakker, the punk evangelical son of famed televangelists Jim and Tammy Faye Bakker. Late every Sunday afternoon, he would hold service in a funky, dank bar. That's when his congregants would be getting up after a tough night of music, booze and whatever. He was meeting them where they were. He believed the evangelical message, but he also believed that we are all made in God's image and deserve to be loved. That meant LGBTQ+ as well, though megachurch pastors like Joel Osteen beg to differ.

Bakker was interesting. His parents had resigned from

their evangelical TV and entertainment empire. They had become the poster couple for divine dysfunction – there was even jail time involved. It was a pathetic stew. Jay rose from those ashes to fight for inclusion, and he was shunned for his efforts.

We travelled from one end of the country to the other in fourteen days before ending our journey in Denver. It was the Democratic National Convention and America was about to nominate the first Black man to lead a major party for the presidency. The city was buzzing. We decided to go out in the street and interview whoever caught our eye.

I spotted one fifty-ish couple wearing "We're Jewish Republicans" T-shirts. I asked them to have a seat on a downtown park bench with Democrat partisans lining the street. It was a parade-like atmosphere. I asked why they supported the Republicans. The party was leaning very heavily on evangelical support at the time, as it still does. "They're good to Israel!" they said. I asked if they were aware of the evangelical reason for the party's support of Israel. Their hope was that the Jews would return to the promised land and trigger the start of the tribulations. This would then lead to the apocalypse, where those who did not take Jesus as their Lord – in this case the Jews and Muslims, to say nothing of the poor atheists – would be knee-deep in their own blood, their souls thrown into the fiery pit of damnation. The believers fared much better – they would be pulled from their graves to celebrate the return of the Messiah.

The man looked at me with an impish grin. His wife piped up: "Look, what do I care why they're doing it? Tell you what, if Jesus comes down from the sky and he's the Messiah then hey, he's the Messiah."

I didn't show it, but I was mad. She was proud of her opportunistic machinations. She was an Israel-at-any-cost Jew. I have always worried that if the ends justify any means then we will have a deeply hollowed-out prize to show for thousands of years of exile.

The year before I had travelled to Israel to do a series called *My Israel*. At first, I didn't want to be on camera; I wanted to have people tell us their story. Their Israel. The network, VisionTV, wanted me to be in it. I differed. Perhaps the wounds of twenty years of public life had left me shy of the spotlight, but in the end they were right. The show was much better as a personal journey. I started the series with my mother. I asked her to bake one of my favourites, bizcochitos de miel – honey cookies. I asked her why we, unlike so many other Moroccan Jews, immigrated to Canada instead of Israel. She didn't miss a beat: "Why should we go from being treated like dirt in Morocco to being treated like dirt in Israel?"

I was proud of my mother at that moment. She had taught me one thing that I have always cherished – speak some form of truth to power. Or in her words, when I was older, "Don't take shit from anybody." I have tempered that sentiment as I've struggled to be more compassionate. I've tried to know what hills to die on and when to see it someone else's way. That is more in line with what my father instilled in me.

But, in this case, my mother was airing a grievance that many Sephardic Jews had and still have to this day. We are mostly the Jews of southern Europe, the Balkans and the Arab world. Sepharad. Spanish descendants of the expulsion from Spain in 1492. Basically, 1492 was only a good year for white Catholics. For the Indigenous populations of the western hemisphere, and for the Jews and Moors of Andalusia it was a disaster.

If you go to southern Spain, where many of my ancestors

are from, you will see churches that were once mosques and, sometimes, synagogues. For a time, three of the world's great religions came together in peace. It was a golden age for all three faiths. I wish that Jerusalem today could reignite that flame of unity and truly be a beacon of tolerance, spirituality and peace. But that day in my mother's apartment, the conversation was not nearly as sweet as the delicious cookies she had made.

She was right about the history of the Sephardim in Israel. Israel is a western European construct; it's the result of the Zionist movement that convened in Switzerland and conceived the plan for the creation of a Jewish homeland in Palestine. Jews from Arabic countries were not given prominence in that grand project. When the colonial powers loosened their stranglehold on the Arabian Peninsula and the North African Maghreb, there was a great surge in pan-Arab nationalism. The resurgence was led by Egypt's Gamel Abdel Nasser. In Morocco, the transition to independence was for the most part peaceful, but what came with this throwing off of the French and British yoke was a rise in anti-Semitism. Jews in my birthplace of Tangier were receiving death threats. Many were encouraged by European Zionists to immigrate, to make aliyah, to the new state of Israel. There would be housing, opportunity and most of all, for the first time in millennia, safety in the biblical homeland.

Nonsense. In truth, we were brought there to increase the population, left on border areas in tents close to malarial swamps. Second-class citizens yet again. Years later, when I did the *My Israel* series, we happened upon a spontaneous street demonstration by a group of Sephardic Jews in south Tel Aviv who were protesting their eviction from government housing to make way for new, privately driven condo tower developments. Whenever I would show this series to Jewish groups back in Toronto, one Ashkenazi in the crowd would inevitably stand to say that that's the way things used to be and that the conditions have changed now. I would respond with what one protestor told me – that nine out of ten judges in Israel are Ashkenazi, and to show me where there are Sephardic Jews depicted on the currency. How many prime ministers have been Sephardic? The reply would come; names of Sephardim that had "made it" were recited. I replied, "If you can name the ones that made it, there can't be that many. How many European-descended Jews have 'made it'?"

My mother carried that wound, as do I. We are prone to this disease of particularism. The need to contract into hives of identity and ethnic cause. Duality over unity. As my spiritual path grew, I realized some fundamental truths. One that I still live by is that God is not Jewish, I choose to be Jewish. When I offer that thought to others I am often met with real surprise. It is a thought that many haven't considered. God, Allah, Christ, Vishnu – these are particular ways of understanding the constant flow of cosmic creation. I was moving away from the particular to the universal.

Later in the filming of that same documentary, I was at the Kotel, or as it's commonly known, the Western or Wailing Wall. We were filming me mediating at the wall. It is common practice to insert a prayer or petition into a crevice between the mighty bricks that stand as testament to the longevity and sorrow of the Jewish people. It is a remnant of the Second Temple. It has been fought over, pissed upon and conquered many times over by all three Abrahamic faiths. To me, it is as much a testament to dysfunction as anything. I also believe in the wisdom of those in Judaism who say that the worship of idols cheapens the wonder and awe of creation. Today we have many golden calves that we kneel before, be they money, fame or power over others. The Wall, to me, is also a physical structure that people are willing to pray for, even kill for.

With all that freight, and knowing that my departed father had inserted a prayer in this ancient wall on the one trip he made to Israel before his death, there I stood. I stood and was thinking about him when suddenly I heard someone over my shoulder say, "Hey. You Jewish?" I opened my eyes to see a man in classic Orthodox garb: black long coat, white open-collar shirt, black kippah and forelock. I was not happy. "Yeah," I shot back. "That all right with you?" It soon became apparent that he was hitting me up for a donation to the cause of keeping him at the Wall to interrupt people like me who had come from halfway around the world to have a quiet moment. It was kind of like a prayer tax, and as my friends the Rollers back in DC would say, I was ripe for the picking.

He asked me where I was from, realizing he hadn't quite buttered the bread as well as he should have if he wanted to garner a few shekels. I soon discovered that he was in fact, like me, Moroccan. I was shocked. Usually I could spot a Sephardic Jew at the Wall or anywhere else in Israel by the fact that they did not dress, as the Orthodox did, in the shtetl garb of nineteenth-century Poland or Lithuania.

I felt I was looking at someone who had gone over to the dark side. We Moroccans were a traditional people, but we didn't have gradations of observance – you're either in or you're out. I have come to appreciate the Ashkenazi forms of choice, but that day I was looking at someone who had made themselves over in a way I did not recognize. With cameras rolling, I said goodbye. No money changed hands, though I felt a little poorer for the exchange. The series was a cable hit, garnering Allan and I a Gemini nomination. It is still today played on streaming services, and sadly much of what we encountered – the bitterness, the cries for dignity on all sides and the passions that this tiny patch of arid land enflames – have not changed very much at all.

The years brought me new experiences in politics, some good and some quite disappointing, whether with the Green Party or with my good friend the Honourable Glen R. Murray, who served as a cabinet minister in the Ontario Liberal governments of Dalton McGuinty and Kathleen Wynne, Canada's first openly gay woman premier. Glen, by the way, as well as being the greenest politician in government, had been the first openly gay mayor of a major city in perhaps all of the world when he served in Winnipeg.

My time hosting a jazz radio morning show was coming to an end when I left for a communications job with Glen. My relationship with my boss and friend, Ross Porter, who had done so much to create a viable, vibrant jazz station in the highly competitive Toronto radio market, had become badly frayed and we were no longer enjoying each other's company. Doing three seasons of documentaries focused on spirituality had also deepened my yearning to explore more of not just my Jewishness but my soul.

Politics and soul were not the best fit, as I would soon find out. I had spent many years covering politicians through a current affairs lens, so I thought I knew what retail politics were about. I had counselled Elizabeth May before she gained office, so I thought that I had a real leg up. I was wrong. This game being played in the halls of what is known as the "Pink Palace," Queen's Park, the seat of government in Canada's most populous province, Ontario, was all about power – who has it, who wants it and what either will do to get or keep it.

This was a kingdom of workaholics. Thirtysomethings scurried through the halls typing furiously on the hottest cell on the market at the time, the made-in-Ontario BlackBerry. Even Barack Obama had one. Newly minted politicians arrived believing they could make a difference. Many were soon crushed under the wheels of the leader's office, and edicts flowed like manna from there to the various minions/members of provincial Parliament who were there to stand and cheer on command for their team only, screw the rest.

Consensus had almost no place in the legislature that we all lubricated with worm-on-hook press releases and witty and withering tweets meant to chip away at brand loyalty to other parties. They say that politics is show business for the ugly, and in a way it is. These often-well-meaning types who mingled with the take-no-prisoners operatives in their own parties, while always wary of the hunting press, were also always wondering if and when a knife might come their way, be it in the front or the back. Like showbiz, some rose to the occasion, others to their level of incompetence. The press and public held little sympathy for their fate.

We have demeaned public service and demonized the press that covers them. The theatre of politics plays out while in cabinet members' boardrooms, lobbyists representing those with the money to influence real laws and regulations press the flesh and ply their trade of influence peddling. Many of them have parlayed their time in politics into that very seat at the table.

At times the transactional nature of the game overwhelmed me. One day I was asked by a higher-up if I had returned the call of a certain businessman. I said that I hadn't. "Get on it," came the rebuke. "He's a very good friend of this office and we don't want him to think we've forgotten about him." I was working for the Liberal Party, but I was not and never have been a Liberal supporter. That didn't endear me to some – I kept saying "you" and they wanted me to say "we." But it was not going to happen. I was there for Glen. I did find it ridiculous that the Liberals and the NDP behaved as if their policies and desires were a million miles apart while their common foe, the Conservatives, benefited from their wasted energy. Consensus, compromise and collegiality are tools of the weak. The strong, meanwhile, choose the bludgeon.

When asked, I still advise the politicians I respect, but when I left Queen's Park I looked back over my shoulder and what I saw was a broken system of male patriarchy, adversarial gridlock and a profound tone-deafness to the society that struggled around them. Pink Palace indeed.

My escape hatch came in the oddest form. Because of my Ryerson days, by this point decades in the past, I found myself invited to lunch with an old classmate who I barely remembered. After all, I'd been a good eight-to-ten years older than him when I attended. He was now president of a major Ontario college and I was working with the Minister of Training, Colleges and Universities. He asked if I would like to work with him as his executive advisor. Yet again I was going to have to fake it till I made it. Yet again I jumped at the chance, thankful for the opportunity.

The college was Sheridan, known around the world for its school of animation, and with over twenty thousand students in campuses in the west Greater Toronto Area (GTA) – Oakville, Mississauga and Brampton – it is one of the big five colleges in Ontario. The goal was for Sheridan to become a university. The obstacles were many – classism, parochialism and flat-out competition for both dollars and students. This was going to be, like politics, as much about power as anything else.

I loved the job and was always aware that I, someone with five years of post-secondary experience but no degrees to show for it, was now often in a room filled more and more with PhDs. It made me aware of two things: first, that we live in an age of credential inflation, where a Bachelor of Arts is the new high school diploma; and second, class divide between applied education and research.

The fact that Sheridan already had numerous Honours BA programs and that it was the first school in Canada to create a curriculum around creativity that favoured critical think-ing, quality ideation and novel solutions to existing problems seemed to carry no weight with politicians, and certainly not with other competing educational fiefdoms. Something else occurred to me as I walked the halls of second-tier academia: We were sending these students out into a world that I believed was heading in the wrong direction. One that more and more knew the price of everything and the value of nothing. Inaction on climate destruction alone was going to gift them a dystopia that they seemed, for the most part, oblivious to – partly be-cause of the immortal rush of being young, and partly because they had been conditioned to believe in a neo-liberal, me-first world view that only asked that they pick a lane, the right lane for who they really are and what they should ask of this society.

One day I was visiting the trades building to discuss a potential partnership opportunity with the dean of trades. Sheridan was not a big trades school; it was more arts and high-tech oriented. I asked him why more students weren't interested in the high-demand, high-wage jobs that trades offered. He told me about the parents that came to the faculty with their children and would pull him aside and say, "He's not that good at school but he's good with his hands." He would always smile at them but really he wanted to dress them down. He wanted to look them in the eye and say, "You're telling me that your kid is not that bright? What makes you think he won't build a house that will collapse, electrocute himself on a job site? Fit the wrong pipe and poison a living space?" Trades, he said, were about being a precise and careful creator who, when confronted with unforeseen problems, could have the wherewithal to come up with a great solution. And if class wasn't enough to drive home the process, the gender split was daunting, to say the least, for women looking to be welcomed into the program.

The facts are clear – it's parents that drive the post-secondary bus in terms of stream. If you went to university, it's very likely that your kids will, too. No-degree families often produce no- to low-degree kids. All this and that nagging feeling that while education is sometimes profoundly impactful, it also sometimes deadens the dreams of many a student.

Still, there were so many great people and stimulating conversations that I enjoyed trying to help this group with their university objective. Of course, the other colleges had no interest in seeing us succeed and leave them behind, the universities couldn't have been more elitist and the provincial government saw no political advantage to granting us the new assignation. I trundled from office to office, through mayors, ministers, horribly boring Canadian club luncheons, an orgy of business card flashers and bar mitzvah–grade lunches followed by the crème of the establishment puffing like peacocks at the lectern before we all, bloated and bored, returned to our offices, trying to remember who had handed us which card.

Looking at the cluster of carrels filled with good people asked to do so little but what the office assembly line required of them sparked a sadness in me, and the spiritual longing that I had been struggling to contain started to demand more. I made the decision to move my family out of what had become the megalopolis, by Canadian standards, of Toronto. I felt that life there had become soulless. Too many people scurrying about in a fierce competition for money, resources and time. Dead-eyed subway travellers, drivers who would never let you in because they had been on the road for forty-five minutes already.

I took to explaining to my Friday night Sabbath dinner guests that I felt our city had a "God Hole." That scale had rendered us more heartless. My wife was much more reluctant to move, but I would be closer to work and she was in a career transition. When we informed one of our boys that he would be attending grade five in a place called Hamilton, he wailed and wailed. In the end, though, he says he's much happier here.

But it was more than relocating that was being asked of me. As Jon Kabat-Zinn said, wherever you go, there you are. Over the years, I had often researched pathways to becoming a rabbi. I wasn't ever able to convince myself that with my poor command – as in almost none – of the Hebrew language I would be accepted by any institutions. I realized that I had been looking at these websites for more than twenty years. And every time I reasoned that I couldn't take the five years off it required, or that I wouldn't be able to bear the weight of rabbinical obligations. But here I was again, taking one more look.

There is an ebb and flow to my spirituality. When the tide is in, I am awash with feelings of unity and find that the doorway to my compassion opens just enough to let in the beauty and sorrow of this existence. The triggers vary for this openheartedness. Sometime it's the approach of our highest holidays and the call to reflection, repentance and service. Other times it's my own sadness or despair for the plight of so many for so few reasons. I, for instance, find myself occasionally crying for the earth that sustains us. The hardened heart of our "every man (and I do mean man) for himself" culture. Ironically, we prop up the billionaires not because they understand us but because we hope that through them we can ourselves become rich, powerful, immune. Upton Sinclair, the American writer, said it well: "It is difficult to get a man to understand something when his salary depends on him not understanding it." John Steinbeck, another American dissident writer, has been paraphrased as saying, "Socialism never took root in America because the poor see themselves not as exploited proletariat but as temporarily embarrassed millionaires."

My soul wanderings are not the kind that will make me a religious scholar. I don't know how many angels dance on the head of a pin. So, what was I doing staring at a screen and wondering if I should take one last poke at the rabbinical piñata? I returned to the form of Judaism that has always been aligned with my disposition, Jewish Renewal. A movement that was born of the hippie days of West Coast America. Its founders were well grounded in Orthodoxy and yet had found a way to infuse the cosmic gut punch of psychedelia and the mystic traditions of the Hasidic movement into a new-age Judaism that spoke to those that yearned for more mystery and less certitude.

From that form of Judaism emerged rabbis like Shlomo Carlebach, "the Singing Rabbi"; Arthur Waskow, the leading proponent of an Earth-based Judaism that reconnected Jewish teachings with stewardship of the planet; and, most impactful of them all, Reb Zalman Schachter-Shalomi. With books Like *Paradigm Shift* and *From Age-ing to Sage-ing*, Reb Zalman brought a magical synthesis of classical and profound Jewish practice and tradition into the twentieth century and now beyond. He asked questions like, "How do you get it on with God?" He launched a dialogue with the Dalai Lama that was captured in Rodger Kamenetz's wonderful book *The Jew in the Lotus.*

I was hooked. As a teenager, I was a tail-end baby boomer. That meant I could only see the Earth-based and communal experiment of the hippie generation from a distance. I was too young to participate actively but old enough to attach myself to the utopian ideals that were launched in the face of a dour and war-addicted Western world rife with cruel "isms."

God as mystery, people as beings – all beings – infused with a spark of the divine that could be activated by the connection of one heart to another. The teachings, seen through the lens of unity, took on a rich meaning for me that never truly left. So here I was, scrolling down the course curriculum for a place called the ALEPH Ordination Program. There were choices: rabbi, rabbinic pastor – never heard of that before – and finally, Hashpa'ah, or Jewish spiritual direction. I gravitated toward that, the one I could do while still providing for my family. I applied only to realize later that I had missed the last line where they said that you had to be enrolled in the rabbinic stream to apply. I wrote a second note saying that I had missed the fine print and thanking them anyway.

The next day I got a reply asking me to hold that thought. A decision had been made that this year they would accept people who were not rabbinic candidates. I would be interviewed. I was excited but also felt like I would get laughed out of the virtual room. We spoke – actually I spoke, a lot, to two different rabbis. I waited. And, eventually, I was accepted.

How was this going to mesh with my home life in a new city? I was going to be the only Canadian in the program and would have to travel to Colorado every six months. What would my president over at Sheridan say? He was, by his own admission, not the kind that pursued such spiritual paths.

So, what is a spiritual director? That has always been a tough question to answer, especially in the Jewish world. A spiritual director, or SD as it's called, has a much more robust community in the Christian world. Accessing the wholeness of the human narrative through story and tradition with a spiritual guide or companion can ground a person in a way that allows them to open up to universal questions with a focus on reflection, contemplation and increased skillfulness. Note that I don't include the word "answers" in the process. It's refining the questions that draws my attention: Why am I here? What purpose could and even should my life have? How do I wrestle with transition, grief and inner peace?

At its core, the process of Hashpa'ah is about holy listening. Hearing with your heart and responding to theirs. We yearn for spiritual connection through the often-broken heart; we yearn to be heard. As I moved through the three-year course, I found a rich cohort of fellow travellers and a growing appreciation, through Reb Zalman's emphasis on deep ecumenism, of all spiritual paths – religious or otherwise.

I do remember how I started on that journey. It was to be a week of face-to-face workshops in Colorado, just outside Boulder. I arrived at the airport in Toronto ready for the flight out. Trouble was, the plane I was expecting to take very early that morning didn't exist. No flight number on the departures board, nada. I approached the desk. It should be noted that I had made a conscious decision to wear my kippah for that whole week. I wanted the world to see that we can all carry faith, and a reminder for myself that whoever saw me and how I behaved would think that I must be what a Jew is. I approached one of the service people and asked where my flight had disappeared to. She informed me that the flight had been cancelled a month ago. Part of me was confused, part of me was relieved. Hey, this could be a sign not to go, even though I don't believe in that sort of thing. I thought, You were just going to embarrass yourself in front of all those people who know way more than you will ever know about being a Jew. Turns out the travel agent had either sent a note that I did not see or just didn't notify me. I asked what I was supposed to do now. Turns out, there was another flight, with connections, that was set to leave in eight hours. I was in a good space by this point, spiritually. I made the choice to be present to what Eckhart Tolle calls "the isness" of my situation. I sat cross-legged in a hallway and brought out a book to read. Time melted away, but my reverie was shaken by an announcement over the PA system. "Ladies and gentlemen, we are experiencing extremely cold temperatures out on the tarmac right now and because of that we are declaring a ground stop. No planes will be departing until further notice."

Okay, so maybe there is such a thing as a sign. I had every reason now to back out. I was supposed to arrive for an opening circle ceremony by 6:00 p.m. Mountain Time. This was just not going to happen. Yet, somehow, I was settling in to my kippah-clad serene disposition. Whatever happened was not necessarily meant to be but I still had a choice as to how I would receive it. By the time I got to the airport in Denver, fifteen hours had passed. As I was standing there, waiting for the shuttle, a woman walked up to me and said, "Rabbi, you look tired, is there anything I can do for you?" I smiled. "Oh, thank you, I'm okay." I loved that moment, but I also knew that I had been misidentified. I began to say, "I'm not a rabbi," but she interrupted and said, "I'm Christian, but I just wanted to say that it's good to see someone like you today. It's been a hard day for me. God bless you." "God bless you, too." For that moment, I had been what that kind woman needed. For that moment, I had been what I needed, too.

I finally arrived at the hotel having missed all of the ceremony. I headed to my room exhausted but somehow peaceful. The trip took seventeen hours. It was worth it, though. A new chapter had begun.

During that week I did a deep dive into a way of relating to others that I had only ever danced around all these years. I had begun to give sermons, d'var Torah, at my lovely downtown synagogue when the rabbi was kind enough to ask me. I could feel the powerful energy of the Torah portions that we were exploring together. For me, Torah is not in any way a literal and cohesive narrative. It is a poetic and metaphorical journey into right and wrong, holy and profane; a chance for us to see humanity, with all its flaws, as part of a greater consciousness. When God is asked, Who are you, the answer is the same in all faith traditions. I am that I am. Total presence.

As our workshop progressed, we realized that we hadn't been called together to become spiritual lifeguards. We were there to become present to what is, and to deeply hear what yearnings the process of spiritual companionship could bring to light in the person we were sitting with. I was glad that I hadn't turned to run that day in the airport. This new chapter felt right.

My time at Sheridan had me feeling well paid and appreciated, but the job was a creative gamble by the president and I always had the gut feeling that I was in a precarious spot. Advisors come and go, but I had always managed to find a way to flow from job to job. The spiritual work did something else for me in my work life. It allowed me to listen in ways that I hadn't before. I was able to bring down my wall of ego, good and bad, and listen with my heart. That didn't mean that I sat like a mush ball nodding away with an insipid grin on my face. It meant that I could accept the energy and concerns of those around me and with compassion, as opposed to ambition, and offer a more measured and useful response.

Take Your Time and Let Us Know

I finished my ordination and began to guide workshops and individual counselling sessions. I had gravitated to one of Reb Zalman's cornerstone projects: Age-ing to Sage-ing. I had crossed the threshold into my sixties, and the area was a rich one for me. I remember the day that so much changed. I had joined the gym at the college to get myself moving. I had never really liked gym culture. Still don't – too much huffing and puffing. That day I had a late meeting with the president. He had announced his departure suddenly and in a way that left many of us feeling that he had always had another horizon in his sights. I was brought into his large office; the afternoon light was soft and the cloud cover was a gun-metal grey. He started the conversation with a joke about seeing me featured in a newspaper article about my family's move to a new city.

"Hey, I know that guy!" Then he got down to the task at hand.

Just about all of us had been let go. There was a feeling – not just disappointment but also shame. What will I tell people? How can I make this look like it was my decision? I should have seen it coming. It made perfect sense if I thought about it. But I had just moved my family to another city. I drove home feeling gutted. What was I going to tell my wife? I love her and my children so much, and I had always seen myself as a provider – the guy who goes out and hunts down that moose. In the face of big moments like this, I usually spend a day or two feeling very sad and then jump back up. I have worn many hats over the years, and I have been nothing if not resilient.

But I was about to embark on a journey that I was ill prepared for. Ironically, it was one that I had started running workshops about. I had entered, or should I say I was backing into the autumn of my life.

I was torn. Should I step back or leap forward into the next big pants job? It would become the most confusing time in my life since my adolescence. Before I could move forward in any direction, I needed to take stock and acquaint myself with all the colours that autumn can reveal. To find a way to understand what society thought of us as we age, and what we must do to reap the harvest of our lives and share that wisdom in a world that devalues aging. A time where life is often reduced to fearful stories of physical decay and personal diminishment.

Changing the Channel

David Cox once compiled a list of the recurring attributes of older characters in film and television for the *Guardian* newspaper. First, let's keep in mind that only 5 percent of characters in cinema and on TV are over sixty. Of those 5 percent, the paper maintains that they are overwhelming portrayed as "ineffectual, grumpy, behind the times, depressed, lonely, slow-witted, sickly, whining, rude, miserly, hard-of-hearing, ugly, interfering, heartless, intransigent, doddering, mentorish, frisky or profane."

Let's stay with this list for a moment and understand that in the face of this overwhelmingly negative menu of aging attributes, we have some decisions to make as elders and for those who will eventually follow us. Looking at this list, I realize, in the vernacular of the age, that this shit is starting to get real.

Intransigent, slow-witted, miserly and profane – what an indictment. For those of us who watched more than our fair share of Hollywood sitcoms growing up, we can call up images of characters like Granny on *The Beverly Hillbillies*, a stereotype wrapped in an even more denigrating stereotype. She was frisky, as pointed out in the list above, inappropriate and often prone to random cruelty. Occasionally she would dispense some Texas wisdom to her son or granddaughter, but mostly she was looking for her false teeth and/or her trusty shotgun.

At best we got *The Golden Girls*, a quartet of high-powered TV actresses brought together after the success of *Maude*, starring Bea Arthur. Even there, Arthur's character had to endure her own mother, who was rude, heartless and interfering. We, it seems, can look up to the old when they come from other cultures, but in the Judeo-Christian frames in which we in the West live, the old are a deeply flawed burden. With the weight of that relationship comes objectification and different forms of dehumanization and abuse.

Perhaps that is what was already embedded in my heart when I met my first octogenarian – my own grandmother. She followed us to Canada from Morocco in the late 1960s. I had grown up with no grandparents – the other three had died in Tangier before I was even born. My grandmother, Mama Camilla we called her, was eighty-three when she arrived. She spoke Spanish and Arabic, and God love her she did not have a single clue as to what in the hell was going on in her new "home." I was unaccustomed to old people, and everything I had seen on TV conformed quite nicely to the *Guardian*'s list. I frankly didn't know what to do in her presence. Her skin seemed more like cellophane, paper thin and covered in spots and discolorations. Her hair was dry and grey, and her teeth were often in a glass beside her bed. The barriers weren't just physical; they were cultural, as by then I was quite Canadian-ized. I had no appreciation of the life she had led. I didn't know that she had travelled from Tétouan to Tangier by donkey and, if I heard correctly much later on, she had miscarried along the way. She was the second wife of a grandfather I never met.

His first wife had taken ill and was dying. He married my grandmother to take care of her as her illness progressed – her, and the five children his first wife had borne him. After the first wife passed, my grandmother had five more children with him, my mother being the youngest of them. We were of very different worlds. As baby boomers in Toronto, we were filling the streets with protest – or at least my sister was – listening to Hendrix and wondering what American Yippie founder Jerry Rubin meant by his cri de coeur, "Do it!" I remember lying there in my room thinking, I would do "it" if I knew what "it" was, or where I could get it. Meanwhile, down the hall, my grandmother sat staring out the window of our first-floor apartment, marvelling at the sight of snow. I ran out the back and got her some. She liked that.

We weren't together in that apartment for that long. Even-tually she was housed in what we have come to call an old folks' home. This one was big, and like most at the time, set up more as a long-term care hospital than the retirement village offerings being marketed today. She spent the next fifteen years there, passing away at one hundred. I hated going to see her there. Not because of what she was going through but because I was scared of the place. The smell of death, the helpless people, wheelchair bound and slack-jawed, moaning into the empty spaces, their eyes searching, scared, forgotten. It was, and mostly is, a warehouse where we send our loved ones. We are enmeshed in the private good – private house, car, cottage, backyard. The nuclear family has become the core of our lives. The common good, indeed the Commons itself, is mostly gone. What place do the elders have in this atomized landscape? What value do we place on our interactions with them?

We see age and physical decay as the singular focus of care. Trapped in our need to remain vital we, as elders, want to give away nothing. Why would we in an anti-aging society? We marvel at the ninety-year-old sprinter and the eighty-two-year-old distance swimmer, but as I hit the official age of "retirement," I hesitate to tell others about this personal milestone. The old have whiskers, the old become invisible, the old become our burden.

The question that arises is one of process. How might we change the channel as it were? Why do we need to see our elders as ineffectual, burdensome and filled with reminders of death? Again, I come to death and our desire to avoid it, especially in those that carry its nearness more obviously. Perhaps the answer lies in which clock we live by. There is the chronological clock that gets its due once a year. If you search your feelings about birthdays, I am sure that much will be revealed. There are those that say, oh birthdays, I hate them, such a fuss over nothing. Others go through ebbs and tides around the day – sometimes feeling that they are where they want to be in life and other times not wanting to mark the passing of a hard year. But the shadow must be given its due. Making it for one more year means moving one step closer to the end, or so it would seem. Here it gets tricky because the end, if one is purely rational, is nothing but a physical event. Approaching the end is an exercise in maintaining the biological unit for as long as possible. But if we embrace a different conception of time, other doors may open. Ram Dass writes: "In the end, of course, our approach to the future comes down to how we feel about mystery. As much as we know about ourselves and our existence, there will always be a great deal more that we will never know. The soul has no problem with mystery at all. Mystery is the Soul's element. As wise elders, we come to know that the ego has no control over anything, and so we begin to rest in the mysterious present and let the future unfold as it will."

Hollow ad phrases like "you're not getting older, you're getting better" reassure us that we can cheat aging and, by extension, cheat death itself. I resented shaving my beard. My youngest son confirmed my defeat upon arriving home from school. He looked at my hairless face and simply said, "You shaved your beard, Daddy, it makes you look young." Old and improved. Just doesn't have a ring to it. Pity, it should.

Which brings me to anti-aging creams and unguents. A group called Transparency Market Research published a report stating that from 2013 to 2019, the anti-aging market grew by 7.8 percent and was worth 191 billion USD. Almost two hundred billion dollars! This, by the way, doesn't take into account the figures for getting "work done," as they say in the cosmetic surgery business. In an April 12, 2017, article in *USA Today*, it was reported that seven million Americans receive Botox injections every year at an average cost of 385 USD per shot. Most of those injections were for treatment of wrinkles. Hair replacement, liposuction – the list goes on and the profits are huge. But apparently, boomers have the means, at least in parts of the industrialized world and more and more in the rapidly growing middle and upper classes in Asia. According to this article, 70 percent of US disposable income is owned by the baby boomers, and when it comes to spending on anti-aging products and services they seem to feel quite free to open their wallets and purses.

Of course, the reasons for getting the work done vary. Some do it because they can. It's like freshening up. For others it's a business move. I know one successful business owner who has had tucks to remove the bags from under his eyes, hair replacements that repopulated his scalp and permanently banished any hint of grey, and a nose job simply because he didn't like the size of his old one. The first two procedures, when I asked him why, were about his relationship to his clients. He didn't want to look old. They would start looking elsewhere, assuming he was probably on the way out, or worse, that he was out of touch with the latest trends. He literally couldn't afford to look old. He also had a surgical eye procedure so that he could go without glasses. And you know what, it all worked. His clients stayed loyal. He's seventy-six now and everyone says he looks great.

Putting cosmetic surgery aside for a moment, there are some who believe that an immaculate outward appearance reflects a level of self-respect and is a way to honour God. I remember one of my more religious cousins asking me why I didn't wear a suit and tie to synagogue. I replied that I, like many I had spoken to over the years, felt that the synagogue experience had become more like a parade of peacocks, congregants advertising their newfound wealth and sitting pretty – literally. I am making an assumption, but I detected no connection to a sacred experience as they sat in place; they were there for a presentation that might at least make them feel some contentment.

My cousin wasn't buying my casual dress argument. "If you

were invited to see the Queen of England, would you wear jeans and a T-shirt? Honestly, would you?" "No," I replied, honestly. "So why would you not want to dress appropriately to spend time in the presence of God?" God, by the way, to him, is best imagined as the King of Kings. I never really bought into that version; my path forward required a different spiritual fuel.

But if most of our cultural signposts are pointing as far away from aging as possible, what's in it for us to age gracefully? Just walk by any bus shelter advertisement and look at the face of the models selling . . . whatever – jeans, perfume, travel. They are literally children – heavily made up and often sexualized, but children nonetheless. They are the sirens on the rocks, calling to us. Come back, you were me once, it's yours for the taking. Desire feeds our impatience, but in looking at some biblical outtakes we can get a different perspective: "But the Lord said to Samuel, 'Do not look on his appearance or on the height of his stature, because I have rejected him. For the Lord sees not as man sees. For man looks on the outward appearance, but the Lord looks in the heart.'"

I have never been much on the "Lord said." There is something too transactional, too small about reducing the awe and power of the universal flow to a series of edicts transmitted from the unknowable to my tiny ears. But what I do take from that passage is the idea that when it comes to what connects us to the unity of creation, it is best to look past the outer shell and into the metaphorical heart that we all share. Are we capable of doing that? If not, perhaps I should not overestimate my fellow humans and should "get thee to a good cosmetic surgeon," or at the very least pick up some hair dye.

For me, the challenges of outward appearance have taken on

a different hue. The form of cancer that I hosted had taken up residence in my nose. Funny how we never think much about body parts until they find a way to grab centre stage. In my case, my septum had been hollowed out and the part of my nose that continued after the cartilage had done the work of keeping it up, well, it just collapsed. At least the left side did. After treatment, I had cosmetic surgery, which was only partially successful. It left me looking nasally challenged, if not deformed. I was no longer me, no longer the man my wife called handsome. I took what had happened as a challenge to my vanity, to my sense of the permanence of things. I tried to live with this new face. The one with the sharp dip where my nose should have met my brow. The one with a nose that was now quite thin. The one that made it so I could walk by people who I had known for years and they didn't recognize me, though occasionally they would give me a double take as they passed. I learned to say my name, and still do, as I approach people.

Eventually, with the help of my more-than-kind ENT, who like so many in that field was also running a cosmetic surgery practice, I decided to have another procedure to at least make my nose symmetrical. I didn't take that decision lightly. I waited two years to do it. I was trying to live, in Buddhist terms, with the truth that nothing is permanent. That our looks are not just subject to age but also transformational disease. There is a great spiritual challenge in how our bodies change regardless of when or for whatever reason that change occurs. If this life is transitory then why shouldn't we embrace the changes that come with age? What is it that, looking back over the shoulder of time, could leave me with a feeling of regret? I had a choice – I could regret that I was not what I once was, or I could see that with every breath, with every passing moment there is a small goodbye. With every passing person another chance to start again, not from where we were but from where we are. It is not an act of surrender to inhabit our present tense. It is an opportunity to savour, to be awake, to see who and what is all around and in us at this very moment. I learned something from that experience: Presence is all I have. This very moment. The past is just a collage of images and reimagined moments. The future has not arrived.

But letting go is difficult. We see our pop culture icons as the years go by and we unconsciously wish them to be frozen in time. They accommodate us, popping on our screens with tightly wrapped faces that give our forever stars an almost ghoulish visage, kind of like a dog's face as it hangs its head outside the window of a fast-moving car.

I remember hosting a live television event in Toronto in 2003. It was a concert meant to show the world that the recent SARS outbreak, which had taken many lives and scared tourists away, was over and something not to still be afraid of. The Rolling Stones, AC/DC, Rush and others were trotted out onto a stage to entertain a huge crowd. As the evening wound toward its climax, the crowd waited for the appearance of the headliners, the Rolling Stones. I was positioned in front of the stage, between the crowd and the band. After an appropriate amount of delay, the kind expected in the church of rock and roll, the Stones finally hit the stage. Keith Richards blasted out the opening chords to "Start Me Up." The years haven't been kind to Keith's appearance but he has done little to hide its effects. The lights changed, the sound cranked higher and Mick Jagger strutted out to his microphone. His hair chestnut brown and long, his body lithe and athletic. The crowd went wild.

I felt like I was watching a Rolling Stones cover band. That I was at some casino where rock bands go to pasture and we relive our youth as we gladly accept the disconnect between who is front of us and whether or not they are singing with their real teeth. The Stones have been in my life from the beginning. As a small child I sat with my family, parked in front of the TV on Sunday nights to see them on *The Ed Sullivan Show.* As I looked up to the band from the lip of the stage, I wondered how Ronnie Wood could still have not a strand of grey in his mop of rock star hair. Now I wonder, why did we need him to look that way?

One member of the legendary Rolling Stones did not play the forever-young game. I had the chance to interview drummer Charlie Watts some time after the SARS concert while working for JAZZ.FM91. Mr. Watts, along with being a member of the band, is also a big band leader and jazz aficionado. His collection is cross-referenced, mammoth and highly nuanced. He came down to our modest radio digs one day when the Stones were rehearsing in Toronto. They often came to the city to get their show together in an empty airplane hangar at Pearson International Airport.

Charlie was a gentle and unassuming man. His hair was grey, his eyes still twinkled, but it was clear that no "work" had been done. In fact, he had done nothing at all to upgrade his aging body. He was tasteful and, frankly, gracious. There was something peaceful about the evenness of his voice. He had settled into a relaxed rhythm that it seems he had warmly embraced many years earlier. I don't think it's a coincidence that Mr. Watts was both comfortable with his place in the journey of life and loves and plays jazz.

I'm not saying that jazz has some magical power – though it does – but in the years that I hosted a jazz program, I came to realize a few things about the people who play it. They don't do it because they are going to get famous, or rich. For most, the crowds are small and the pay is smaller. They do it because they have to. It is in them and it must come out. They have to have a level of musicianship that only finds its parallels in the classical musics of the world. The other part worth noting is that one can grow old in jazz with no need to recreate the adolescent hormone rush that fuels so much pop culture. A seventy-two-year-old pianist can sit in the pocket of this rich and spiritual music and just play. Suit and tie, or jeans and sweater. No matter. Jazz ages well. The ravages of time make it whole. Charlie Watts knew that.

We all approach age differently, I suppose, but spiritually one has to wonder if anti-aging creams, chin tucks and Rogaine make the path easier or if they are simply a form of fairy dust we sprinkle around in hopes that others, if not ourselves, will be assured that we are not changing, that we are still here. But perhaps we are looking in the wrong place to validate our journey. Perhaps life is not measured best by cheating death, at least outwardly. In *So That Your Values Live On*, edited by Jack Riemer and Nathaniel Stampfer, there is a chapter from a young man named Eldad Pan. He was a twenty-year-old Israeli soldier killed in the War of Independence.

> Lately I have been thinking about what the goal of life should be. At best, man's life is short. His life may be kind or harsh, easy or difficult, but the time passes before he re-alizes it. An old person wants to live no less than a young

person. The years of life do not satisfy the hunger for life
. . . precisely because life is short and no one can completely
enjoy it (for we die with half our desire unsatisfied) [Eccles.
Rabba 1:2], therefore we should dedicate life to a scared and
worthy goal.

Eldad was young when he wrote this and died soon after,
but what I admire about him is that he realized that age had
little to do with purpose, and I'm sure has even less in common with our desire to keep our icons, and ourselves, forever
young. Ask any actress in Hollywood about the availability of
work once they reach the tender age of thirty. We yearn for the
maiden, tolerate the mother and, it would seem, mostly hold
the crone in contempt.

The Buddha also asked us to consider that longevity is
perhaps not as important as what we do with ourselves in the
time that we have. He said: "It would be better to live for one
day wise and meditative, than for a hundred years stupid and
lacking awareness. It would be better to live for one day full
of vigor, than for a hundred years lazy and idle" (Dhp. 111–12).

But popular culture has, at times, another face. Older, aging
and ready. There are some who, as they come to the end of not
just their careers but their lives, bring a powerful spiritual element to their last hurrah. Johnny Cash, the legendary Man in
Black, recorded one more time before his death. In full knowledge of his end, he collaborated with producer Rick Rubin.
Rubin told him of a televangelist who claimed to have cured
his own cancer by taking daily Communion. Cash had Rubin
find his old Communion kit and he said it every day, often with
Rick witnessing him, usually over the phone. Johnny ended

each call by saying, "I love you, Rick." And Rick would love him right back. The first song they released on that last album was a beautiful lament. The song is called "Help Me." It opens the collection, the last he'd ever sing. In it, Cash speaks from a humble heart, he begs for help and bends his knee toward his God. We have an opportunity in aging to move from ideas of winning and losing the battle of life, to moving toward the Communion to which Cash was drawn. To unity and humility in the knowledge that we are not alone, that we are part of something bigger. Indeed, we have never been alone.

Listening to Cash sing this song, your heart breaks. Unlike Jagger, who defies his age with every concert, Cash sits quietly in the recording studio with a tired voice, the Man in Black gone grey, his frail voice reaching out from soul to soul as if to say, Take me home, Lord. It reminds me of a ritual pet peeve of mine. In Jewish prayer, there is a point in the service where we are to go into silent prayer. It's called the Amidah. Part of the ritual is to be standing with your feet together and body upright. For as long as I can remember I have resisted putting my feet together and often lean on the bench in front of me instead of remaining upright. I know what I'm doing – I'm refusing to sit in my humility. I will stand any way I want, and slouch, too, damn it. It's become a thing for me, and about me.

A small smile breaks across my face as I position myself for this prayer cycle. It lasts about five minutes. I have stopped reading the words as quickly as I can in Hebrew. Most of them don't mean anything to me. Instead, I push my feet together, put down my prayer book (the Siddur) and close my eyes in silent meditation. I often find myself contemplating my family and sending them love and compassion. Perhaps now, finally,

I'm slowly arriving in the moment as my ego gives way to my true self, my soul.

Like Cash, Canadian icon Leonard Cohen went in to the studio to leave us with his last will and musical testament. I had the pleasure of interviewing Cohen several times, for radio and television. On one occasion I had a good half-hour to spend with him. I asked, "So, you're a Buddhist now, right?" Cohen looked up, "No, I'm not." "But you just spent six years in a Buddhist monastery." Cohen paused and said, "I'm a Jew. We have within every religion all that we could want or look for." The key, he said, was to build a fence around the sacred in our lives. To cultivate the garden of our spirituality and to tend it well. With his masterpiece, "Hallelujah," Cohen cemented his place in the spiritual life of so many people around the world.

As a septuagenarian troubadour, he proved that a performer can show their age and still electrify an audience. As he approached his death, Cohen did not retreat into issuing a collection of his greatest hits. Instead, he met his end with the grace and audacity that were his hallmarks with his incredible "You Want It Darker."

Hineni is the Hebrew for "here I am." When Moses encounters the burning bush, he bows his head, removes his sandals at God's command, to feel the sacred earth beneath his feet, and says, Hineni. Here I am. For me, the central question of faith is not where is God, it's where am I? What have I done to make myself available to all that is around me?

If God is process, then aging must be part of the flow – the shefa. Yet we live in a cultural milieu that gives little value to process, let alone age. If we are to take our cues from the grossly under-represented elders in our cultural media, then there isn't much to look forward to. I spent most of my adult life in media, but there came a time when I'd had enough. Instead, I worked to help others communicate messages that I thought people needed to hear. When I did appear at some event it was like I had risen from the ashes. Seeing the surprise on people's faces, I would pre-emptively say, "I know what you're thinking: 'I thought he was dead.'" My provocative quip was often met with a quick denial, but I don't think we can help it.

I think that perhaps we need not be so absolute about our choices. We can find a way to steer clear of the cartoon decrepitude that populates our less-than-inspired storytelling and imagine the autumn of our lives differently.

The Japanese have no word for retirement; instead they focus on ikigai, which I would call kavanah – your profound connection to your intention. For the Japanese, getting in touch with their ikigai can mean that they remain engaged and eager to continue doing the things they love, truly love, for the rest of their lives. According to *National Geographic* reporter Dan Buettner, a long-time student of Japanese culture, we all have ikigai deep inside of us. It is the ability to locate our true inner voice, that which calls to us but is so often obscured by our mostly fear-driven operating systems. Once we're caught in our fears, we become reactive, compulsive and unable to hear that voice, the one Judeo-Christian's call the "still, small voice," above the din that we ourselves cultivate. Growing into our sage-ing years is our last best chance to hear what for many is a voice that they have never learned to listen for.

Perhaps the old fool sitting quietly on the front porch is not so ridiculous after all. To hear what is all around and available to us requires stillness. But in a culture where stillness is often looked down upon, that can be hard to do.

The Japanese also believe in cultivating moai. This is the coming together of people with shared interests that do something important. They look after each other. According to Buettner, moai came to be because farmers would get together to share best practices, especially in hard times. Today we have virtual communities where elders can congregate online. This can be helpful in breaking down the walls that we seem so determined to build around those that are getting older, but I wonder if high tech can be of profound use without high touch.

I first heard that idea, high tech versus high touch, at a lecture given by educator Walter Pitman when I was at journalism school in Toronto. He maintained at the time, in the mid-1980s to be precise, that the advent of more technologies that allow us to connect to each other should not fool us into believing that our more intimate forms of collaborating could be duplicated. He wanted us to find ways to enhance our people skills, not just our tech touch. To me, he was talking about the heart to heart that is the cornerstone of not just social but also spiritual life.

Spirituality is about relationships, as is life. If the dying repeatedly tell us as they are leaving, that it is all about love, then what good is a chat room unless it is underpinned by the body heat that is at the core of what we starve for?

In an article detailing the impact of social media on loneliness, author Sherry Amatenstein writes:

> We've all been in a public place, waiting for a friend to arrive or simply dining, traveling, or sitting alone, and opened an app to avoid "awkward" eye contact with those around us. And it is common for social anxiety sufferers to open social media apps to temporarily feel some connection to others. But when they unplug, the feeling of connection dissipates.

Furthermore, frequently viewing curated snapshots of other people's lives might leave social media users feeling as if *everyone else has a better life, is smarter, funnier, more interesting, has more friends, etc.*

Connecting virtually can benefit us but it can also make avoidance easier. How many times do we decide to text or email rather than call or visit someone? We have gained "connectivity" but have in some ways lost community.

What I'm talking about is what the Buddhists call the "third treasure." The first treasure is the Buddha, which signifies the unity of all, the web that we are all part of as explained by Vietnamese master Thich Nhat Hanh. The second treasure is the dharma, which through the teachings brings us a skillful refinement that shows us the beauty and wisdom of the diversity of all things. And then, finally, the piece that we as elders must strengthen if we are to survive the pressures of marginalization, the sangha, the community where unity and diversity come together.

I remember sitting at our Sabbath table one evening, with ten or twelve people gathered together for our feast. One new attendee, a good friend, was seated beside me, and as the conversation and wine flowed freely we rested in the twilight of the day. It was time to claim some space. To leave the doing behind and simply be, together. My friend was a distinguished academic and former university president. Jewish by birth and temperament but an avowed atheist – a scientist, as he put it. He was playfully jousting with me about my belief in God, telling me that his religion was the pursuit of truth. There was nothing to refute there, but as I looked around the table,

I turned to him and said, "Science is to me the articulation of the mystery and a crucially important pursuit. One that can banish ignorance and calm the superstitious mind. But there is one thing that science cannot give you."

"What's that?" he asked.

I turned to the table and all the animated discussion and sharing going on, and said, "This."

We smiled at each other, and he said, "Well I can't argue with that." Thich Nhat Hanh understands Sabbath as well: "We will be more successful in all our endeavours if we can let go of the habit of running all the time, and take little pauses to relax and re-center ourselves. And we'll also have a lot more joy in living."

We can and do find ways to connect to each other through technology, and much good can come from that, but what religion has given us cannot be easily replaced. The opportunity to congregate, to watch each other grow up and through this life. The ability to witness each other as we mourn, celebrate and come together to share life's journey is one of the greatest gifts that we can partake in.

Growing older can be lonely. It's often experienced in a segregated space, such as seniors' residences, retirement communities and, in my neighbourhood, an adult daycare centre, for those "enjoying" their golden years. Two-thirds of Canadians live in suburban communities – places where the car is king. The streets are often four lanes wide each way and the average speed . . . well let's just say it's the perfect speed for crossing the street if you're on the track team at your local high school. Some streets don't even have sidewalks and the main thoroughfares are often divided into road, sidewalk, thirty feet of grass, a sound barrier and finally subdivision housing where the large, cookie-cutter houses with no backyards face away from the traffic. The setting is not conducive to having people mingle, congregate or even say hello. Now imagine being old enough to find driving too much. Or having some physical ailments that make it too difficult.

Without the car you are lost. With it you could at least get to the mall where you can watch people shop, maybe even do a few laps in retail purgatory. There is no sangha in that scenario.

We have professionalized care of our elders. In Denmark, they managed to create an opportunity for older women to come together, stay in their community and in many cases thrive. They renovated houses in existing neighbourhoods, with high streets in walking distance of the houses. In each home they created semi-autonomous apartments and some common living areas. The women – and it is still women who live longest – had company when needed, felt part of the community and were given the most precious spiritual gift of all: their dignity.

I keep forgetting how old I am when I venture out into the professional fields that used to be my playground. For example, I recently approached a public broadcaster about an idea I had for a current affairs radio show that simply asked: Why? They liked things about it and asked if I would go away and refine the pitch. A few days later I received a call from the very able and creative lead on new program development, a woman close to my own age. She asked, "Do you have to host this?" She quickly added, "Not that you might not be the best host for it, but are you married to that?" I was taken aback. I had hosted many shows over my public broadcasting career and was often well received in that position. I had even been doing some hosting for them recently. I quickly reassured her that I was open to whatever was best for the show and we said goodbye.

That call stayed with me. Whether she meant it or not, I was being told, look you're kinda old and we're looking to change the guard around here. I had often heard people say, well the audience is dying. In fact, though the hosts had become younger and younger, the audience was still overwhelmingly older. Radio listeners are often a fiercely loyal breed. Having me on the air, a blast from the past as some were saying, was not going to help matters much. I asked a friend of mine who hosts a satellite radio show and was once the king of morning rock radio in Toronto if he thought he could still do that high-pressure morning zoo show. "Without a doubt," he replied. Yet there is this belief that elders are stuck in their ways and have had their turn.

Then we get people like American presidential hopeful Bernie Sanders, white-haired, in his seventies and the darling of the young. Why? Because there is something universal in what he articulates. Social justice doesn't have an age limit. Universal health care isn't just for the elderly. We have so much to share as we age. I began to think more and more about the spiritual questions that aging brings up. Where do we put those ideas in a society that doesn't seem to care about the big questions?

I'm Spiritual – Not Religious

In North America today, roughly one in five say that they are spiritual but not religious. But a 2017 *Vox* article points out that "almost 20 percent of Americans, according to a survey . . . by the Public Religion Research Institute (PRRI) belongs to a category that transcends stereotypical religious identity." It goes further, reporting that, "by contrast, 31 percent of Americans identify as neither spiritual nor religious." These respondents skewed younger and more educated than the religious Americans, with 40 percent holding at least a four-year college degree and 17 percent having some form of postgraduate education.

It may be important to ask what else we might lose if we lose our religion. Now, let me be clear: many people leave religion behind for what they, and I, believe are the right reasons – intolerance, bigotry, toxic exceptionalism. Add to that dried-out theologies and patriarchal structures. Religion can be all those things. But, frankly, any social organization can be that – the army, the steel plant, a rock concert, you name it. The flaw is in the human part. What concerns me is the loss of connective tissue and the creation of a safe space to ponder the mysteries of existence and the struggle to become ethical beings. When people tell me that religion is the root of all evil, I ask if soccer is a close second, given the fanatic and sometimes violent culture it engenders in parts of the world. As Leonard Cohen said, we must tend the garden. Leaving our sense of connection to only what can appear on a laptop – FaceTiming with the grandkids, Skyping or Zooming with old friends – might be something but it also might not be anywhere near enough.

If we are to have a cogent response to the marginalizing forces that demand that we and those we admire never age then we must turn toward each other. Otherwise we leave that space not just to technologies but also to those that offer care, at a price.

We have chosen to live in atomized family units, and even connecting with our neighbours in the adjoining house or apartment has become too much. As for family, we are mobile, we leave our parents. On average, in bigger cities people move every three or four years. The social investment is, well, I'm not sure where it is anymore. Perhaps it extends no further than our fenced-in yard or a twelve-foot-long concrete balcony.

As we age, we will have to elbow our way into the mainstream dialogue and look to each other for support, and to find deeply meaningful ways to connect, to mentor and to stay engaged in all that still calls to us. Thirty years ago, the image that terrified so many of us was that of the frightened senior furtively perusing the supermarket aisles, stocking up on tinned cat food – not for any pets, mind you, but to be hoarded for their own consumption. We were all going to end up destitute. Now, apparently, we're all going to end up on a cruise ship, flashing credit cards at the next exotic port of call. Truth is, for many poverty is still very real.

All of these scenarios are grounded in our desire to cling to what we have constructed; to the personality, material inventory and never-say-die pictures we create for ourselves. But what of the soul, that other element that I so clearly saw leaving the body of my father almost thirty years ago?

I defer to Thich Nhat Hanh again: "The cloud will never die. It may become rain, or snow, or even ice. It may change shape, sculpted by the westerly winds but in essence like the soul itself is an eternal piece of the web of creation." Even the atheist can find common cause here. Energy, as physicists say, never dies; it may transform, but it is eternal. Perhaps the Richard Dawkinses of the world view my belief in the soul as mere vanity. Or worse, a weakness that propels me into cult-like positioning that will not accept the finality of this biological unit. I can see their point, yet I prefer to dance a little pirouette, luxuriating in the mystery that I can't deny is all around me, around us. There is little room for this garden of the soul in a culture obsessed with the individual and their buying power.

In fact, the majority of magazine and media literature aimed at seniors keeps driving the demographic lower in hopes of adding just the right amount of honey to aging. The better to attract advertisers to the good life fantasy they can offer in return. There is a magazine in Canada called *Zoomer*; it is part of an overarching media and financial services strategy that includes an oldies radio station, a classical music offering, a high-gloss magazine and a television station populated with classic Britcoms and *Murder, She Wrote* reruns. The group also owns CARP (formerly the Canadian Association for Retired Persons). Its counterpart in America, AARP, represents, lobbies for and offers insurance and other products to over forty million members. I recently picked up a copy of *Zoomer*. On the cover, ridiculously enough, was Canadian celebrity Jason Priestley, best known for the retro TV hit *Beverly Hills, 90210*. I have nothing against Mr. Priestley, and by all accounts he is a very talented director as well as actor, but the idea that he was staring out from the cover of this magazine as a representative of someone in their later years, an elder, seemed, at least to me, quite cynical.

Zoomer has over the last ten to fifteen years steadily lowered the "senior threshold" for its marketing purposes in hopes of grabbing a piece of the thirty-four to forty-nine buying demographic. Get fit! Look great! At the very least dye your beard, will ya! Fun factoid: getting rid of the wrinkles in your neck costs about thirty thousand dollars – zoom that.

There is a story told of a billionaires' bacchanal on Shelter Island. Reportedly, two of America's greatest modern authors – Joseph Heller of *Catch-22* fame and Kurt Vonnegut, who penned *Slaughterhouse-Five* among other great titles – were standing around as the lights danced across the room, the liquor flowed freely and the glitterati, well, they glittered. Vonnegut turned to Heller and said, "Joe, how does it make you feel to know that our host only yesterday may have made more money than your novel earned in its entire history?" Heller replied, "I have something he doesn't have." "What could you possibly have that he doesn't?" asked Vonnegut. And Heller replied, "I have enough."

This story has been with me long enough that I'm not sure of its veracity or if it is indeed apocryphal. Regardless, it speaks to a notion that is essential to spiritual growth – the decision to deal with our attachment to the belief that material pursuits will make us happy. Anthropologists call it the "good life fantasy." Just one more thing, that's all I'm asking. One more car, house, shirt, shoes, wife, Facebook friend. Now, as we enter the autumn of our lives, we are asked to continue the fantasy, continue feeding the shadow of want and the vulnerability that comes with it. We whiten, we brighten, we flaunt our buying power. We become seniors, active, productive and still in whatever game best suits the householder mould building the modern-day cave to protect their young and vulnerable family. But if we are to enter the forest of contemplation on this journey, we must first come to terms with changing the value proposition that no longer fulfills our needs.

As our levels of desire change, so too must our world view. Again, I factor in our repulsion with the inevitable – the fact that we are going to die and that none of those things we've acquired will be useful for the journey ahead. We will not be burying our servants alive with us, and no, clay soldiers are not needed to protect us. At times like this it helps to see how others view what we insist is the end. In *The Tibetan Book of Living and Dying*, Sogyal Rinpoche speaks to another possibility: "For what happens at the moment of death is that the ordinary mind and its delusions die, and in that gap the boundless sky-like nature of our mind is uncovered. This essential nature of the mind [what some religions locate as the heart centre] is the background to the whole of life and death, like the sky, which folds the whole universe in its embrace." The audacity of that claim in the face of clear-eyed rationalism is, in my opinion, worth exploring.

I spoke recently to a close relative who was eloquent in her belief in the place of mystery in her life. She kept apologizing for her "flaky" views. I tried to assure her that she was in good company and encouraged her to flake away. I am quite comfortable with mystery and enjoy a deep dive into it, but she kept apologizing anyway and I understood why. After all, we are rewarded for proof, even in a life where we lie in rich and often non-rational dream states each and every night. We spend our waking hours in a state where memory is nothing more than a construct, where love is pursued with no proof of its existence, where we must apologize for seeming "flaky" when we could instead turn to each other and say, "What a wild ride this is. Spinning at six thousand miles per hour on a miniscule ball in a field of stars that stretches into millions of galaxies. Seriously, this is WILD."

Remembering that many depictions of our elders revolve around the notion of the senile, doddering fool, perhaps there is little in it for us, with silver in our hair, to turn to the person beside us and say, "We're all literally made of stardust, you know. The energy in each of those particles will never die. We go on in some way forever." Now, if this were proclaimed in a movie where the old person saying it was Morgan Freeman and he had just come back from a cloud walk, or by an Indigenous actress in a period piece, we would probably find it enchanting. But if it's the guy beside you at the local chain store, well that, at the best of times, is suspect.

After all, if, as I stated earlier, no more than 5 percent of characters in our cinematic storytelling are over sixty-five years of age and the vast majority of those depictions are of inappropriate, demented or mean-spirited seniors, then there isn't much that would convince most elders to stand and deliver. As Zalman Schachter-Shalomi writes in *From Age-ing to Sage-ing*, most people can't honestly say, "Yes, I want to be an elder when I grow up." Homer, he points out, shows Odysseus as a world-conquering hero returning from his mid-life adventures, but we never see him harvesting his wisdom in his later years. Lear, well, he just descends into madness, destroys his greedy children and dies after his royal power is taken from him. Lovely life lesson, don't you think?

We celebrate victory but rarely honour the wisdom and peace that comes with reconciling our relationships and opening ourselves up to agape, the soulful, loving and generous heart of someone who knows that we are one with creation. Is that flaky?

As elders, we have a chance before we leave this mortal coil to renew our purpose. If we now live longer than ever before in human history then maybe we can burn our bingo cards and stay engaged with others and with ourselves. Aging is an opportunity to cultivate love and appreciation for the mystery and gift of this life.

Love – To Hold Dear

It's hard to know when we've crossed certain bridges in life. I haven't encountered any "aha" moments that changed everything. It's more a bits-and-bytes-style accumulation of seemingly disparate shards of knowing and unknowing. As the years unfold, I have found it easier to invite more mystery into my life. Entering my autumn with more clarity, I realized that I had to out myself. I had to start using the G-word more liberally.

Sometimes when I talk about that four-letter word, God, people pull out their trump card. "Prove God!" they shout. I, and others I've heard, always answer the same way: Prove love. Can you hold it, buy it, put it in a bottle? No, yet we spend our lives searching for it, holding onto it, watching it change and sometimes letting it go. Love, like faith, is something we do, not something we can clutch in our small hands. One phrase that does confuse me, though, is "God is love." In my eyes, God is not encapsulated in human emotions. Besides, if God is love then is it also not hate, fear, hope and death? I'm not looking for a one-dimensional presence. So, let's uncouple God from love. Let's not prove or disprove but instead take a dive into human love.

There are so many destinations for our love. We don't just love people; we can also love nature, service, justice, food and – as the Old Testament implores us – we can, we must, love the stranger.

When it comes to getting older, it seems that the type of love that gets the most attention is sexual love. The literature is everywhere about seniors' sex. The premise is that as much as younger people find the idea of old folks rubbing bodies together, even achieving orgasm, repulsive, older people still want sex and young 'uns be damned. It's almost an act of defiance to hear some tell it. I don't deny that sex for older people is important, but I want to broaden the idea a bit. In the context of a sexually repressed culture where sexuality, like so much else, is a commodity – a currency, if you will – we are in danger of framing the sensual lives of our elders in the same superficial way that we categorize all sexual activity: performance, power (or the lack of it) and the potent rush of a chemically enhanced flow of blood to our primary sexual organs.

"Sex is better than ever," we hear the octogenarian say. That may well be true, but is it the same sex that we had in younger years? Should it be? Does it need to be? What about those who find that sex doesn't have the same hold on them anymore? Call it a lust deficit. As a young man, I was overwhelmed by the hormonal rush to procreate, to feel lost in the power of intercourse. Should I feel that way now? Perhaps occasionally, but also perhaps not. I imagine for some it's a relief to move from copulation to companionship. To feel the warm and soothing touch of a loved one that says you are touchable, love-able, still here. Love as we age has something we can't acquire before its time: a narrative. Our stories are of love found, lost, nurtured and forgotten.

I do not exclude myself from the expectation that we must be forever sexy. I have trouble letting go of the high-performing ideal. It feels like surrender somehow to bob around in the low tide of slower sexuality. I sometimes fear that low tide is my new normal. That by accepting it when it comes, I've lost something that I've relied on to feel good about myself for all these years.

I would say that contrary to the crass stereotype of the dirty old man, I feel that as an older man I am more respectful of women than I was as a young bull. I appreciate the same things, in my case in the heterosexual frame that I work from. But these days I am able to be in the presence of women without the same longings I once had. It's liberating and I now see the person in front of me more clearly. But perhaps this calming of the storm happens regardless of who is or isn't in our lives. The challenge I face, and sing along if you know the words, is to blend passion with a new piece – wisdom. Sexual wisdom. Marvin Gaye spoke of sexual healing, and maybe entering into this phase of life is a chance for us to do just that, to heal ourselves. What would it be like to enter a new realm of sexual grace, one where we are not fixated on performance over connection?

We celebrate, often with good reason, the people who marry and stay together for forty, fifty, even sixty years. But for most of us the reality is that one spouse outlives the other, or perhaps divorce ends a relationship. I, like many others, have had two marriages, and from that I have learned a great deal about myself. For instance, we live longer and we can start again even if we marry for long periods of time. How do we cohabitate over all that time and commingle is the next question to be answered.

Even so, there is a great imbalance, as far as gender goes, that can make finding a mate in one's later years difficult. For instance, women live on average eight years longer than men, which eventually leaves seven women for every man in places like assisted living retirement communities. Even then, while 55 percent of women are unmarried, only 28 percent of men are single. Basically, single women outnumber single men by roughly a two-to-one margin. What is it about us men? We can't seem to fathom the idea that we might have to go it alone. Lord knows we talk a big game about toughness and self-sufficiency, but leave us out there on our own for more than eighteen months and we curl up in a ball on the La-Z-Boy watching *Family Feud* reruns. A *Globe and Mail* article from a few years back pointed to a new wrinkle: women, or at least two-thirds of them, preferred LAT – living apart together – to getting married and cohabitating in their later years.

An American survey came up with the top dating sites for people wanting to find the next Mr. or Ms. Older. Sites like MillionaireMatch, Friend Finder and Senior Black People Meet. I found the specificity pretty hilarious, but what really caught my eye was the use of the word "friend." It's not that older people don't want sex; it's that they want it with a person who can offer them that and more. Companionship. They may even just want the friend part when it comes right down to it. Getting older means you often accept who you are more easily. This is not the time for stumbling through relationships driven by a mix of hormones, dreams and a healthy dollop of immaturity. This is the time to fold into the soft creases of life with someone who, like you, has lived, loved and known that with love we must accept that there will be grief and sorrow as those that we love and have loved pass. For after all, the price of love is grief.

I know a woman who in her late eighties, after years of living without a husband, found and fell in love with a man who had already turned ninety. He had outlived two previous wives and, like many men, quite quickly went about the business of finding a new one. They lived quite happily together for about five years until he died. I always enjoyed seeing him with his arm around her shoulder as they smiled and laughed with family. After some happy banter he would excuse himself and go for his afternoon nap. It was lovely.

My mother lost her husband, my father, while in her early sixties and never seemed interested in remarrying. We did all the things good children do – we told her that we had no problem with her finding someone to share the rest of her life with. Thing is, she'd had several suitors over the years, and that was enough for her. "I've been taking care of people my whole life. The last thing I need is some man expecting me to make him dinner and keep him company." She was content to see some friends at the synagogue, watch lots of the news on television and indulge her long-neglected passion for painting. Her apartments since have always been filled with her creations. Was she always happy and never sad or lonely? Of course not, but she was living life on her terms and that was as it should be.

As I write this, she is alone and frail in a long-term care

facility far from me but close to my siblings. She is ninety-six, and one thing I can say with certainty is that she is not online dating. She seems content with the attention of her children, or as content as she can be.

With this long lifespan comes a fair amount of baggage, but if we allow ourselves to unpack some of our emotional carry-on we can see that some of the "faults" we have ascribed to others when in failing relationships was really us. Here's one advantage to having more than one long-term relationship – when you have a second or even third life partner, you start noticing if you have a habit of putting off important conversations, or if you are much too quick to anger. You can't help but feel that life is much less about what's wrong with those we share it with and more about what aspects of our own character we have not taken the time to refine. It can be sobering to realize that partner number two is echoing the same complaints about your character that were so well articulated by your first partner.

In the Jewish tradition there has been a revival in the concept of "mussar," a values-based approach to shaping our character through mindful practice. The idea is that talking about being better and more ethical is not enough. We must also reinforce our better traits by consciously picking one trait at a time and taking action that enhances our ability to embody it. Mussar can focus on a trait like humility, order or truth and employ an active and mindful strategy to strengthen it. There are three parts to a daily practice: a morning mantra that is read out loud or chanted to frame the day, a mindful action as one goes through the day and then nightly journaling. The effect can be profound. Alan Morinis's book *Everyday Holiness* gives you a coherent and well-written road map to developing a strong mussar practice.

Imagine, as we re-enter the world of dating and search for new love after fifty, that we pause and first take the time to make sure that we have done the work of being a better partner. That we are not impulsively shopping for a mate out of fear of being alone, as real as that can be. But instead we offer a better version of ourselves that will bring depth to the relationship by being reflective. A morning mantra, a mindful action and an evening journal. Brilliant.

We can choose to enter areas of contemplation on this journey from senior to elder. We can embrace conscious action, even revel in our aging process or, as so often happens as we move through the stations of life, we can back into it, eyes closed, taken by surprise and unprepared to accept the gift that's been offered.

I have heard people complain about the lack of good potential partners out there, but rarely have I heard them say, "I think I'm going to spend a little time getting to a better place myself before I size someone up, or settle for someone, anyone, who'll put up with me and keep me company." Given the rate at which men quickly remarry, I think we would benefit greatly from embracing that pause.

Of course, this is easy for me to say right now as I'm blessed with a loving wife, but I have to say, I find it fascinating that so many more women become self-contained as they age. I believe that women have reserves of strength, physically and spiritually, that men either expend early on or, in the case of spirituality, neglect to cultivate. But fear not, gentlemen – and women, too – there is a remedy. You just have to take a little leap. But as they say, if you do choose to jump you will grow wings on the way down.

Into the Woods

Growing up in a three-bedroom apartment with six people milling about, I always cherished the times when I could actually have the bedroom I shared with my brothers to myself. Sometimes I would place the egg-shaped microphone attached to our honking big Philips reel-to-reel tape recorder in front of the radio by my bed. I would wait for the first few bars of a song, and if I liked it, I would press down hard on both "play" and "record," and basically put together a 1960s version of a mix tape. Only bigger. I would lie on my bed and listen to the tunes, and my mind would wander. Being the macabre sort at the time, I found myself thinking of dying. As the youngest in the family, I could afford to think these thoughts because I figured everyone else would go first. I remember thinking that if there was a God then he was cruel. Cruel to put us here, make us aware of our mortality and then, for no apparent reason, let us die. Die, for God's sake – not have a bad day or even a lousy year but up and die. The randomness, that's what hurt the most. Sure, old people die, I thought, but so do innocent bystanders, people doing wonderful things for mankind, children – even children. It's a bloody outrage. Why put us here in the first place? And if you must have us drop in for only a short visit, why make us conscious of life's limitations?

My cats and dog have every Buddhist practitioner licked. No pun intended – I hate puns. Those creatures are completely present, with no awareness of their eventual death. They are content to literally putter about, sleep, eat and occasionally run around. Ironically, their relatively short life spans often teach our children some of their first lessons about love, attachment and that inevitable price we pay in grief when they die.

When first touched by the hand of death, I, like so many, had done little to prepare. I had not rehearsed my dying so that once faced with the prospect I could enter into that journey with some measure of grace. Within my own faith there is an acknowledgement that one dies many small deaths in a lifetime. Every year, on the day of atonement, Yom Kippur, we are to dress in the white cloth that closely resembles the funeral shroud that they will one day wrap our bodies in when we are emptied of our soul. The shroud will cover us from head to toe and we will be buried within twenty-four hours in the simplest of pine boxes. The body, as Ram Dass says, becomes an empty spacesuit that we once inhabited on our eternal journey of impermanence.

Every night Jews say a prayer that speaks to tying up loose ends: the bedtime Shema. We forgive those who have wronged us, whether intentionally or accidentally, and ask forgiveness from those that we have wronged. We do it with the belief, at least for those like me who revel in the mystery, that life is composed of a multitude of deaths. You see at night, so goes the teaching, we don't just sleep; our souls ascend and become part of the eternal flow of God or, as I and others like to call it, the Shefa.

When we wake, our first blessings are those of gratitude. We are grateful that our souls have been returned to us so that we might live another day in our ongoing quest to become a mensch – literally a human being. I know in the age of reason this seems like a fairy tale, but I for one deeply value and bend my knee to mystery. I'm not speaking of the paranormal; I am thinking more of awe and wonder.

Matthew Fox maintained that the Church had become too Jesus-centric, that religion had left behind the awe and wonder that gave the spiritual journey its humility; that gave us the ability to be available to the magnificent, unimaginable power and majesty of the cosmos. Perhaps that is why so many scriptures speak in terms of kings and lords. Yes, these are unequivocally and unjustly patriarchal, but in their time, they were attempts to capture, at least in the Jewish tradition, some powerfully infused shards of what is truly, for the human mind, unknowable. Fox did not shrink in the face of his chastisement. Instead he incorporated many spiritual elements from Indigenous beliefs and other deeply ecumenical sources in an exploration of wonder and awe he calls Creation Spirituality. One river, many wells, as he would say. Since discovering his work, deep ecumenism has become a passion point in my learning.

Occasionally, I have been asked to give the sermon, the d'var Torah, by my rabbi. I have taken the honour seriously each time it was offered, and tried my best to bring the story, or parsha, of the week into a new and interesting light. One week I decided to play a little bit. I had learned an icebreaker in my years of public speaking: "I want you all to turn to the person nearest you who is not a spouse or family member," I said. "Pease ask them in the next two minutes to tell you the story of their name. You are not to answer or ask questions when they speak. Just hold what they are saying and listen from your heart. When they are finished, please reverse the roles."

The sanctuary was abuzz. People were animated, and I knew that they would never look at the person they were sharing with in the same way again. That they would have an intimate piece of another's life inside them. That, too, is love. Then we went downstairs to share food in the Sabbath communal meal, Kiddush. This time I felt like we could go a little deeper. Not much, but a little. So many of us in that synagogue basement had been coming together for years and still knew so little of each other. Not even each other's names, let alone the life that they, and I, were living. Watching this unfold made me realize that what I needed to be part of was something more spiritual than religious. That without the spark of intimacy and relationships both within and between each other, I could practise religion without investing my deeper heartfelt self in its rituals. Rituals that for me and so many have become dried out. I smiled and moved a step closer to creating that intimacy.

Since then, every autumn I gather with a group of eighty to one hundred men at a Jewish retreat centre in Connecticut. The weekend is called JMR – simply, the Jewish Men's Retreat. What happens there is rare for us as men. Unlike the bond of war or crisis, or of sport or commerce, we come together to sing, dance, sweat, share and pray. The traditional Sabbath service is turned on its head. For some, it is their first chance to see the service as a truly joyous thing and to take a chance at making heartfelt connections. It can be quite scary to see some men get up and dance in the centre of the sanctuary – hands up, arms intertwined as they form a circle. I have taken both my eldest sons to the retreat. As the younger of the two and I walked toward the service, I said to him, "Men are going to get up, jump up, and lose themselves in joy, but you don't have to do it just because they do." I don't get up and join in the dancing. I play a djembe, an African drum – it's the gift I feel most comfortable in offering. What we revel in at JMR is often called Jewish Renewal. It's a movement that mixes east and west, mysticism and traditional practice in a stew of intimacy that brings out good things in people. In this case, in men.

This strain of Judaism has its roots in the Hasidic movement that blew the sensible barn doors off of Judaism about 130 years ago. Every religion has its ecstatic branch. This one includes the cult of personality, teleporting rabbis and the usual patriarchal trappings of every orthodox religious grouping. But sometimes, by releasing the grip of rationalism, we can transcend the need to have everything fit into a neat little box. We can take the leap of courage needed to conquer our separateness, to break through the firewalls we spend so much time constructing. Embracing this idea has been my leap into a radical acceptance of the role of mystery in my life. It probably explains my aversion to spreadsheets as well.

In this men's gathering, we are mostly older and feminist, but with a good sprinkling of younger men to offset all the greying beards. As an older man, it has truly been a gift to have either of my first two boys at these retreats over the years. It hasn't happened very much and I have always been careful about pressuring my sons, all four of them, to follow my path. Their lives are mine to nurture but not direct. For those times when they have occasionally accompanied me, what I hope they saw was men being intimate with each other, reflecting on their roles as men and building their emotional vocabularies by sharing their journeys. It's courageous, when I think about it, actually bringing a loving intention to our gathering and daring to feel love and loved. Growing up takes guts, growing older makes the task more urgent.

As we prepare to leave the retreat, some words of wisdom are imparted to us about the bumpy re-entry that awaits. If we have a partner, we have to remember that they weren't on this journey. They didn't enter the sweat lodge with us or share their trials and fears in small sharing circles that formed three times during the weekend. We might have a glow that frankly others find annoying as we re-enter our homes. You know, the "Glad you had a great time, the dog ate my shoes while you were gone" welcome. Kind of a buzzkill. Still, each year I am able to bring a little bit more in the door to sweeten my love for my family.

The love I leave behind informs the love that I pay forward. I have been in two twenty-year relationships now. I have loved badly and well. I have learned that if there is unhappiness it is most often because I am not cultivating the source of my own love and gifting it to others. I have loved some friends and lost others. I will always remember my childhood best friend leaving the hospital with a surgically altered throat and tongue, eking out the words, "I love you." He caught me by surprise. We had been engaged in the sterile world of doctors and timelines up till that moment. But he didn't want to waste any more time with them. He knew it was better to speak his truth about all our years growing up together. I got in my car with a clutch in my throat and tears in my eyes. We were forty-three, he and I, at the time. He died only a few weeks later. I will always love him.

Take Two Teaspoons of Agape and Call ME in the Morning

If you want the moon, do not hide at night. If you want a rose, do not run from the thorns. If you want love, do not hide from yourself. – Rumi

So, how can aging make for loving better? If you believe, as I do, that the spiritual journey is grounded in our relationships – to ourselves, to each other and to our awe-inspiring universe – then follow me down this path for a while.

As we grow older, we have a profound opportunity to cultivate the most precious element of a good life: love. Who have we loved and who loves us? What are we going to do with that knowledge and how can we repair, or at the very least enhance our loving relationships?

It requires courage, as do all things that deepen our experience of this life. Honesty as well. If I think back on my failings in loving my partners, my children and my friends, it is much easier to look away. Easier still to lay blame at the feet of others. But as we age, we can take a different path. One that gives us clarity and new opportunities for renewal.

The courage to love comes in many forms. For this couple, after many years together, it was about choosing life. From Terry Doyle:

> Mary and I had a couple of special moments in our later years. When I was first diagnosed with cancer and told I only had a few months to live, the radiologist in Sudbury said that they couldn't promise anything but he wanted me to do six weeks of treatment. I had gone through that with other friends, and they were sick and vomiting every day. I said if I have to go through that to extend my life for a few more months, I'd rather not. His next argument was that he might be able to save my life but I probably would lose my voice box and my tongue. At that stage, with Mary in the room, I said I think I would rather go home and die.
>
> This is the love part. Mary agreed with me. I was sure that she would have tried to talk me into putting up the great fight but she said, "It's your decision, if you want to go home, we'll go home." I loved her at that moment probably more than I ever had, and I remembered that when she wanted to die last year . . .
>
> The night of the twenty-fifth, about 3:30 a.m. after I had fetched a hot compress for her neck pain, she said in a clear,

young voice, "I'm so lucky to have you." (I have to tell you, I am softy crying while I type this.) That was the most tender moment of our fifty-six years, and at that time I had expected her to live for years longer.

For some, getting older is a chance to bring more love to a relationship with one or more of their children. I had a client in one of my Age-ing to Sage-ing men's groups. He was a successful lawyer and had a son who lived in Brooklyn playing jazz and barely getting by. Their relationship had always been strained. I had asked those in the group to write a letter to someone they loved, a letter that their loved ones could read after they were gone. This man, this lawyer, chose to write one to his son. He did a lot of things in that letter. Said things that required introspection, humility and courage.

He realized, he said, that he had never really accepted his son's decision to be a musician. He could have been, should have been a lawyer, like his dad. Would have done well at it, too. He could have lived the good life. What he realized in writing the letter was that he had devalued his son. Undermined him, really. He was sorry and he said so. He read that letter to the group of men in the workshop. It was a powerful moment for us all.

When we reconvened the next week, he told us that he had phoned his son. He'd told him that he was sorry that they weren't closer and asked, with sincere interest, how things were going in Brooklyn. No offer of money to help out just a genuine interest. It took a while for his son to let his guard down but in the end, they cried a little together and ended their call with a simple, "I love you."

The writing of that loving letter was something I learned

along the way from one of my rabbis. She called it the "Oh my God" letter. She writes one for each of her four children every year. If and when they hear that she has died, she says, they can blurt out, "Oh my God!" then go to her filing cabinet in her home office and find a letter waiting for them. A letter filled not with advice and regret but love and blessings. It's a powerful tool for unlocking all that's left unsaid. As Hillel says, "If not now, when?" To do this work is to go about the business of cleaning the container of our lives. A container that is often filled with regrets, lost connections and even frustrated dreams. It's not an easy well to look down into, but if we are to move with confidence into our eldering then we must open our hearts to all, even that which is so much easier to push into the dark recesses of our souls.

Love Me, Love Me Not

As I grow older, I have noticed that for many, love is often a form of currency. Something to be doled out if conditions are met. Something too precious to offer to just anybody. In fact, even in relationships with those who we profess to love the most, we can twist our loving into something more akin to a carrot or a stick. To protect ourselves from hurt we sometimes weaponize love. Yet once we leave the interpersonal realm of loving it seems that love changes. You'll often find clergy saying that God is love. The dying person often says that all that matters in their disappearing life is love. Love becomes more universal in its meaning, more generous in its application.

During the holiest day of the Jewish calendar, Yom Kippur – the day of atonement – we have a ritual that requires much of us. It is called the Viddui. As we list the darker things that we have done – the lies, the pettiness, the hurtful acts – we knock on our chests. We are breaking the hard shell, the klipah, that we spend so much time building around our hearts. We do this because only through the broken heart can we access our spiritual selves.

I do believe that there is a difference between naïveté and open-heartedness. Is it wise to offer love to everyone? Most of us don't believe it is. Doing so means that we lack boundaries, or worse, that we will be crushed by love. But what if we see it differently? What if instead we offer love, not under condition of an equal and opposite offering but simply as an act of grace and generosity? If I don't need you to love me back, then every-thing changes. To be clear, this takes guts to do. It's safer, if not sadder, to keep our armour on.

Don't misunderstand, I'm not offering this because I have in any way mastered it. I can mutter ungratefully about some-one who has wronged me with the best of them. I'd love to be Saint Ralph instead of the terribly uneven ball of contradic-tions that adds up to the unfortunate total Ralph that I am.

Is it my attachment to a result that stops me from loving and from being available to the love that clergy are referring to when they say that God is love? Well, if I take my own advice, I remember that to evolve spiritually it's best to jump into the spiritual workout room. One way to do that is through a daily regimen of loving intentions that involves gratitude, forgive-ness and courage. By articulating what we are grateful for we can soften our hearts. By forgiving those that have in some way harmed us we can go deeper into this human moment.

Why should you do that? I like the saying "revenge is the poison we drink in hopes of killing the other person." In other words, life becomes toxic when we hold on to hurt and dig deep into ourselves for those weapons that can get the job done: hate, anger, cruelty. I believe that each of us creates the tone of our own narrative. Again, are we a healthy cell in the celestial body of creation or are we cancerous?

As we age, we can choose to do some prudent life review and soften the edges of our personal story. We can a find a way to speak from love, taking the chance that we will be heard and become part of a better story, one we can share with others.

Another gift of living longer is that you can sometimes see how those we have known have evolved. Often, in my experience, it is for the better. That hurtful verbal bully you knew in elementary school could become a good man. I speak from personal experience here – not as the bullied but as the bully. Gather 'round, kids, it's time for a Ralphie tale.

At one point in my first marriage I moved back into the neighbourhood where I had grown up. As a matter of fact, I moved into the house that my old best friend had lived in. His parents, who I had grown up with and loved dearly, had died, one after the other in the span of a little more than a year. I offered to buy the house from him and his sister. They had all been like family to me. He died of cancer within a year of me moving into that house.

The reason I bring this up is that while dropping my kids off at my old school after we had moved in, I bumped into someone who I had gone to that very same school with years before. I'll call him Rob. I was glad to see him. He shook my hand, hard, very hard – it hurt a bit. Then he looked me in the eye and said, "You were really mean to me when we were kids. I never forgot that. Whenever I would see you on TV, I would think about that." I was gutted. Speechless, really.

He let go of my hand and we parted ways. I soon discovered that he had a store in the neighbourhood. I knew what I needed to do. I went to see him in the store and waited till there were no customers around. "Rob," I said, "I heard what you said and I just wanted to say that I am truly sorry for the way I behaved. Really, I can't tell you how sorry I am." He accepted my apology. Over the next few months I saw him several times and each time I couldn't help myself and apologized all over again. Finally, Rob said, "Ralph, it's okay, I just wanted you to know so that I didn't have to see you in the neighbourhood and carry those old feelings around. Please stop apologizing, we're good."

Forgiveness, his forgiveness, mattered. I offered no rationalization for my schoolyard taunts; I lived with what I had done. I had created this situation, and this encounter was an important and natural consequence. As time has passed, I've tried to be a better person. He helped me do a little of that work – he had offered me an opportunity.

Without forgiveness it is hard to take the steps needed to allow us to move forward into love. Forgiving ourselves can allow us to be open to the actions of others. One of the most valuable things I learned in my brief sojourn into acting happened during my brief tenure in the University of Alberta's acting program. Before I hung up my dance belt and scuffled back to Toronto with my thespian tail between my legs, I was lucky enough to hear this from my acting teacher. I don't remember how we got there, but we were in scene study class and two people had just finished a scene. They were good, but there was something missing. A certain authenticity.

Our teacher got up and spoke about inhabiting the characters completely. To do that we had to accept something hard – we had to accept that each of us is capable of doing absolutely anything. We are strong, terribly weak, honour-bound liars. We are capable of killing someone with our bare hands. Literally. As the Yom Kippur prayer says:

We lie
We cheat
We steal . . .

Now this may seem the opposite of what happy affirmations we are encouraged to recite as we start our day – the all-accepting pep talk that is intended to have us looking on the bright side of life. But I'm of the mind that we have to embrace our awfulness. I'm not talking self-flagellation here, though for some that seems an oddly satisfying way. I'm asking you to explore humility. Here's an example. You know that moment, the one where someone cuts you off in traffic or won't yield the right of way? There you are, in your car, growling about their stupid selfishness and wondering what the hell is wrong with people anyway. Cut to three months later. You have been stuck in traffic for forty minutes just trying to get to the expressway on-ramp. Someone catches the corner of your eye. They're trying to merge into your lane. You stare straight ahead – you can't let them in. You've had it with this bloody traffic jam, and besides, you're already late. You are now the bad guy.

Imagine something much worse, someone attacking someone you love. What would you do? I would do anything to stop them, including killing them if need be. Imagine, finding a great pair of winter gloves left behind on a park bench – bonus, right? Could I become a killer if the stakes were high enough, a thief if no one was looking? How do we move from being situationally moral to being the kind of human being we want others to see us as? It's a balancing act. We can strive to be a truly decent human being and also forgive ourselves for failing in the attempt. But the thing is, we still have to try, really hard and with intention – with kavanah.

There is a practice I ask workshop participants to engage in, a guided meditation focused on forgiveness. I ask them to think of someone in their lives that they are having trouble with. Not too much trouble, but someone they can't see forgiving right now. Then as we settle into the meditative state, I ask them to imagine a golden light flowing from their hearts. A golden light of love. As they visualize this, I ask them to think of that person and send that unconditional light to them. Bathe them in that loving light expecting nothing and knowing that you need not engage them or their actions in any tangible way. Just send them love. This is a powerful thing to do. It changes the toxicity of your soul. Forgiveness is not letting someone else off the hook; it's letting yourself off the hook. Giving you permission to get on with your journey without the rocks of hate in your knapsack.

These guided meditations can allow you to do important work. During my Spiritual Direction training, there was an exercise that I found challenging. We were asked to study the Jewish way of engaging with angels. I was asked to present on the topic. I didn't want to. I really didn't want to. I didn't think angels were something I could take seriously. They were right up there with unicorns on my "give me a break" list. Angels had wings and chariots, for God's sake. But I had to do it. Our rabbi took us through a guided meditation that had us journey through the worlds of the four archangels. When it was over, I was stunned by the emotional impact of what those angels represented. I shifted my perception. Angels were energy not form.

Today the archangels work for me as touchstones. I have even adopted my own guardian angels – they are the essence of my father and my old best friend, Mike. They just seem to slip into my thoughts sometimes when I let my mind wander. As I write this, I can see rationalists like Richard Dawkins, the renowned atheist, sneering as he pats my head. There, there, little man, this need for fairy tales shall pass.

But it hasn't. Instead they have become part of my spiritual fitness plan. It might be important to note here that in Christian literature, the four becomes seven. Added to the list are Saraqael, Raguel and Remiel. In Kabbalah there are ten. I'll stick with the four.

To begin, I sit quietly. After a few centring breaths, I let go of my breathing and just observe it. No judgment about the level of stillness I can achieve, I just sit. Then I begin to journey. On my right is Michael, the angel of love and protection; on my left, Gabriel, the angel of strength; ahead is Uriel, the angel of vision; and at my back, Raphael, my namesake, the angel of healing. I slowly traverse the circle of these realms. Love, strength, vision and healing. As the time passes, I sit with each of these qualities and observe what comes up, without judgment. There are no wings or white robes, just a chance to contemplate. To see my imperfect journey through the lens of love, strength, vision and healing. Occasionally I have to admit that John Travolta as the chain-smoking angel Michael does pop into my head but that too shall pass.

A while back, late-night talk-show host Stephen Colbert

had Keanu Reeves on the show. Reeves has spent most of his career as either a romantic lead or a goth action figure. This night, he was goth, dressed in black and promoting another movie. Colbert set him up: "Let me ask you, what happens to us when we die, Keanu Reeves?" The audience, hip to the persona Reeves has cultivated over the years, roared with laughter, waiting for a *Matrix*-like answer. Reeves took a deep breath and answered, "I know that the ones who love us will miss us." The answer stunned Colbert, who was reduced to simply shaking Reeves's hand as they went to commercial. The clip went viral and people started claiming that Keanu was their new religion. A simple and genuine answer, for at least a moment, punched through the pop culture bubble and left us feeling human.

Eldering: The Way Forward

I have often felt that we are here to refine our souls. That, animated by spirit and tempered by intellect, we have a chance to be better this time around. I remember once watching a South American film at a long-ago film festival. It was part of the world cinema retrospective that year. In it, people are portrayed as souls that can stay in the spirit realm or choose the harder route. From time to time they dive off the clouds and into a new earthly life. Not an easy decision because as souls they are not burdened with the suffering that accompanies mortal life, gifted as we are with consciousness and how finite it is. Life in our present form is filled with suffering.

In the film, two lovers leap into love as they have before and will forever across multiple lives. Their love is always different but also the same. Sometimes they are brother and sister, or mother and child, husband and wife. Each leap is another journey into heartbreak and profound grace; another opportunity to refine their souls. To be, to become, to love. That willingness to forge ahead with at least this mortal end in sight will take courage.

In the Mussar tradition, the work of articulating the shape and contour of one's soul revolves around the development and refinement of our character traits. The soul is not looked upon as simply a part of us. It is us. In totality. There are three tiers to this idea: the neshama, which is the source, the light if you will, that suffuses everything; the ruach, which defines the spirit and energy that animates the soul; and finally, the tricky part, the nefesh. One learned rabbi described nefesh as clouds that can either block or give way to the eternal light of the soul. The difference lies between the clarity of kindness, loving kindness, and the clouding that reduces that noble trait to sheer sentimentality. Think of it as the kindness we extend to our children devolving into a permissiveness that leaves them without boundaries and structure that will truly benefit them.

Elder is a role that is consciously chosen and requires preparation at all levels – physical, psychological and, most importantly, spiritual. These are words that I have taken a while to process. Like so many, I drifted into elderhood. Perhaps it's the fact that I, like some, have a second family and sons that range in age from thirty-four to eleven. You can see I have not had the typical trajectory – marriage, children, empty nest, retirement. I often think of a seductive insurance company's ad campaign from years ago, where they promised that if you signed up with them you could drive off into the sunset in a convertible, looking forward to Freedom 55! In my case it looks more like Freedom 85.

Friends often say, "Well I guess having kids later keeps you young." Actually that's not true, it just makes you not want to die. You don't want to let them down, and they still need you . . . a lot!

Richard Rohr says the second stage of life is one that moves us across the bridge from a world where ego propels us in job, career and even marriage, to one that honours the journey and helps us grow into a time of giving, reflection and kindness, mostly toward ourselves. This is not to say that we will live pain free and with an always-open heart. We will lose loved ones. What was once taken for granted physically will often times become much harder if not out of reach. And above and beyond our personal challenges, there hovers still a culture that will do little for us beyond pathologizing and caricaturing us. We will have to claim the mantle of wisdom keepers, wrestle it away from the anti-wrinkle hucksters and cruise ship operators.

I recently heard an online radio host for an "after fifty" broadcast say that he had always felt that he had lost something by not having a rite of passage from adolescence to adulthood. There had been no community acknowledgements, no ritual to confirm that he was about to embark on a new journey, one that left behind some of the magical pieces of childhood and instead asked that he obligate himself to the responsibilities that come with becoming a man. Being Jewish I was reminded that many bar mitzvah boys of my generation began their d'var Torah, a sermon based on gleanings from that week's portion of the Torah narratives, with the proclamation "Today I am a man." Though that wasn't actually the truth it was for some a self-shocking proclamation made in front of family, friends and the community that had seen you born and, in the case of boys, circumcised and running through the synagogue hallways as your parents sat upstairs for Sabbath services. But on this Sabbath, after a year of preparation where you learned to read directly from the Torah scrolls, you donned a prayer shawl for the first time, stood before your fellow congregants and delivered your thoughts for all to consider – on the flood, the Exodus, even the story of creation. This was and is a conscious ritual that affirms that you have arrived at a different place. But even my faith does not have as rich and daunting a path into becoming an elder.

However, many older Jews who were denied a bar or bat mitzvah for myriad reasons, not the least of which was the murderous and hateful slaughter of the Holocaust, have decided to have what was taken from them. An elder's b'nai mitzvah. Working with a rabbi or lay teacher, they may have to do anything from learning how to read Hebrew to the trope, or singing, of what is written on the Torah scroll. Each word has tiny symbols that require the person reciting the portion to have their voice go up or down, the vowels sometimes stretched and others times cut short. Depending on where your people originated from, there are myriad ways to sing this Torah song. The sermon or d'var, well, at a ripe age the words carry much weight and wisdom. The effect on the b'nai mitzvah and the community is profound. But even with this response, we lack something that says we have arrived in a new place. One where we can measure this life in decades, not eternities.

Someone asked me recently about a song that marked a moment of my life. It would have been nice if I had some highbrow response. Miles Davis's "Boplicity," Mahler's Third Symphony. But no, I responded with the Doobie Brothers and

"Black Water." You see, I remember being seventeen in the back of a pickup truck, something I had never done before, with that song blaring out the cab window. I thought I was in love with everything that day – the sky, the fields whipping by, the girl sitting on the other side of the truck. It was early spring and the air crackled all around me. I remember the feeling like it was yesterday. I was immortal, and as we drove down the road my heart was filled with possibilities. That day I realized I could do anything, be anything. As the Doobie Brothers played, with the wind rushing all around me, I was filled with optimism. That feeling informed much of what has fuelled me since. The Doobie Brothers, who knew?

In his book *Conscious Living, Conscious Aging*, Ron Pevny writes about a ritual that comes from Indigenous traditions and has much to recommend itself as we search for a meaningful way to honour the leaves of our lives as they begin to fall. He calls it the Death Lodge; others call it the Life Lodge.

Pevny describes it this way: A Death Lodge is a ceremony in which a person consciously goes out alone into the wilderness in order to lay down some established aspect of their life that no longer serves them. This aspect is released; it receives a ritual death. In sacred terms, this is a "dying before you die," and is one of many deaths that we must necessarily experience in life before our eventual physical, bodily death. The Death Lodge is a way of spending an intense period of time reviewing and fully experiencing all that this element has meant before it is symbolically laid to rest, released into whatever is to arise next in the void that follows the death.

One participant in the Death Lodge entered it a few years back to make real the retirement that loomed before him. He had worked for thirty-eight years and wanted to release himself not only from the day-to-day routines of his labours but also "the patterns and behaviors that had arisen and taken hold throughout this career."

Before we explore the ritual itself, I think it's worth pausing and really taking in what is meant by the patterns and behaviours that arise through our working life. As they say, the hammer shapes the hand. How we see ourselves in the workplace, be it positive or negative, it is a persona that, as we exit that culture or routine, may have little or no place in our next iteration. That may be liberating or, conversely, something to acknowledge and grieve the loss of. Were you employer or employee? Happy in your work or yearning for release?

Let's also look at the importance of reflection and resolution in this stage of not just our careers but our lives. If we are fortunate enough to have lived long enough to reach this stage of life then it is, I believe, incumbent on us to make some decisions.

The very notion of retirement is a relatively new phenomenon that emerged as industrialization matured. It was Otto von Bismarck in 1880s Prussia who first introduced the idea of retirement, under pressure from the socialists that were growing in influence in Europe and throughout the industrialized world. Up till then, quite simply if you were alive you worked, provided you could find employment and were physically able to carry out the task at hand. It took the rest of the decade to create the system that we still have today. A few of the more cynical pieces of the retirement offering ensured that most people would not reap the benefits. Payouts didn't begin until you reached the age of seventy. Back in 1889, that was by no means a given. So, most workers still died in the harness, as it were. Today, with most countries keeping the retirement age at sixty-five, many more people are collecting benefits, often for ten to twenty years or more.

Sarah Laskow wrote eloquently about the rise of retirement in a 2014 article for the *Atlantic* magazine:

> So, roughly a hundred and thirty years ago we decided to help people exit from a life of work, a life that for many was hard, with long hours and the notion of time off or vacations out of the question. As humane as it is to bring us to this place where we can step off the treadmill of work it does present us with real challenges. Spiritual challenges. What have I been doing? Who have I become? Was it worth it? All the compromises, missed opportunities, machinations and the less than tangible results, are these the fruits of my labour?

Even if we intend to continue working after retirement age, it is important to acknowledge the passing of a time, of the summer of our lives where we watched our ambitions, our families, our reputations grow. We identify with what we have created as a work narrative, be it inside or outside the home. But do we have a way of concretizing these abstract constructions?

Let's look at how the Death Lodge experience helped one man deal with these questions – questions that require conscious contemplation if they are not to fester and burn in our souls as regret or melancholy memories. The good old days, or the dream that got away.

> During the first day we prepared ourselves for the solo wilderness experience. In an opening ritual, we picked up a stone that for me represented the burden that I had come to lay down. On the second day, we each set out in

the wilderness of this remote glen to find our spot for forty hours of solo wilderness camping and contemplation, without food.

For the first day, I gave my attention to a thorough review of my professional career: the different jobs I had undertaken. I wanted to sit with the regrets about work – both the things done and the things undone.

I found some uncomfortable truths here around money, security, status and earning.

The questions and insights that arose for this man as he fasted in isolation and focused intentionality were not idle musings. This ascetic approach is familiar. We've seen it before – the image of the Indigenous youth on a wisdom walk, the Buddhist monk renouncing the worldly path and entering into deep humility as they peel away layers of distraction and material gloss. At first, this approach sounds to be at best a luxury and at worst self-indulgent and uncomfortable in the extreme. I know my first response was, hey, you lost me at camping. Fasting I get, been doing it once a year for forty years. Yet, there is a lot to be said for depriving yourself of material life for a period of time. Every spiritual path advises it. This Death lodge visitor ended up collecting work and career memories in a little piggy bank on scraps of paper. He then released those scraps of paper into the river, and then took a hammer and smashed piggy to pieces to rid himself of the baggage of ambition, loss, gain and regret. Then he burned the remains of that little piggy bank in the fire. This was the laying down and the death of his professional career.

The rest of his forty hours in the wilderness was easier without this burden – he had a newfound sense of freedom, spontaneity, generosity, recklessness and presence. It had been a "good death."

There's that word again – "death." Imagine if we honoured all the small deaths we experience instead of just the finite physical one that takes up so much of our thoughts.

But let's bring this down out of the celestial clouds for a moment. Have you ever tried to comfort a child who has lost a beloved pet? As you look into the teary eyes of a distraught four-year-old, they ask in the most genuine of ways, "If Noodles isn't here, where did she go?" So many times, our answer is heaven, she went to heaven. For many this is the white lie that helps their child deal with loss. But what happens when someone dear to us dies? What is our answer then? Is it simply a shrug and a "who knows"? Do we search inside ourselves for a more satisfying answer? Do we wish we could believe, as our ancestors did, that there is a life after death? And that it is indeed a better one?

Whatever our answer, we tend to look upwards for it. Our bias, when it comes to spiritual answers, is to fall back to the childhood answer we just passed on. We ascend to a better place. But perhaps we are shortchanging ourselves. If you walk the forest in late fall you are surrounded by a carpet of dead leaves, rotting tree trunks and moss-covered stones. Out of this fecund array new life grows relentlessly. This time and process, these deaths, the rich soil that a lifetime can create, are essential if we ourselves are to regenerate and move into our wisdom.

These questions have made me a bit of a bummer at dinner parties but that's just the way I roll. I want to explore the path.

If I don't take inventory of where I've been and what I've done then it's really hard for me to move forward. I want the examined life to be part of my journey. That life is often filled with regrets – for what could have been and what I have failed to do or not do. The people I have vowed never to forgive, especially myself. These are not pieces that I have learned to spend time with. This reminds of me of the older man in the retirement home I visited as a lay chaplain. The one so deeply lost in regret.

I saw him a few months later when children from the local Hebrew School came to sing holiday songs for the people at the home. Two of my children were among them. We looked at each other and he smiled. "I remember you," he said. I asked how he was and he took my hand and said, "I'm fine, just fine." I wanted to believe him.

I think about the effect that unresolved regret has on us. Sometimes we just want to stay in that place of damnation. We feel we deserve it. How can we laugh and find joy in a life that is not rightfully ours to live? What this man did not want to consider was that whatever path had led his wife to her death was her path, and that he must free himself of the guilt, blame and shame that haunted his final days. But how do we find a way to do this work?

As Kahlil Gibran says, "Faith is an oasis in the heart which will never be reached by the caravan of thinking."

This quote speaks directly to the disconnect that we feel living in a time when answers are valued more than questions. Indeed, with the ascendancy of science and rationalism, both of which have saved and condemned us in equal measure, we have come to greatly devalue the awe and wonder that people like Matthew Fox stand for. Fox implored us instead to stay confused, to see with our hearts. The great Zen ambassador to the West, D.T. Suzuki, also asked us to leave our logical mind at the temple doors and deal with the "fact and reality" of what is literally present at this moment, not the ruminations that keep our monkey minds so enthralled. Please know that I am not advocating for a life that has us unquestioning and sheeplike. I am instead asking that we reanimate our ability to live with questions that cannot be answered by logic. Why do I dream every night, entering worlds and relationships that I could never concoct in my waking hours? Why does my heart fill with love and sadness when I see the innocence of one of my children?

I have come to believe that if I cultivate the questions of the heart and learn to hear what arises I might perhaps reimagine my journey so that my life can grow richer before I take my final exhalation. I must take the leap toward true vulnerability.

Brené Brown is a fascinating seeker and author. Her life's work revolves around the place of vulnerability in our lives. She uses that lens to understand spirituality in a deep and truthful way. Faith minus vulnerability, according to Brown, equals extremism. To her, faith, a balanced and open faithfulness, is the vulnerability "that flows before the shores of certainty." In my conversations with clerics of different faiths, despite what we imagine, I have not found many who have professed an un-wavering belief in God. Mostly they are passionate doubters. I think that belief hardens like clay in the hearts of those who call themselves believers.

George Roller was a man who, in both his and his wife's beliefs, exemplified what I'm talking about. In his work as a lobbyist in Washington, DC, working on behalf of some evan-gelical Christian groups, he convened prayer breakfasts and organized free "lunch and learns" for the young interns on the Hill – something that these underpaid young men and women gladly took him up on. He was busy and he was good at what he did. George's approach was simple: he would love you into Jesus, and if he was proselytizing it was because he truly believed that in bringing you into the loving embrace of Jesus he would be, frankly, saving your life – and the one hereafter to boot.

When I dined at his suburban Virginia home with a camera crew in tow, the eerily blissful Mrs. Roller serving a virtual feast, I realized that George, or the Holy Roller as he was known on the Hill, had no interest in exploring the mystery of faith with me. He had something he thought was better – belief. Rock-hard certainty that the truth and the light would be the gift, and that he was a simple servant of that truth. There was no searching for commonality. His mission was to drive me toward Jesus.

In all our talk of religion I can say that not one spiritual moment passed between us. Perhaps if I had bent my knee and formed a loving circle with the Rollers as they prayed for my salvation some epiphany might have occurred. That bolt of sudden enlightenment and, as far as the Rollers are concerned, a victory for the faithful and a pledge of allegiance. That is the spadework of an evangelical religion. For me, the work of spirituality is much harder than that. It is about intimacy, not exceptionalism. As Brown points out, we cannot achieve that special relationship with ourselves, with each other and with the cosmology without making ourselves vulnerable.

Many other things can and do come from this type of conviction but not without a deep and often dangerous price. Fuelled by certainty, it is often the nesting ground of tyranny. The "other," and the resultant objectification of "them versus us" feeds on fear, not hope, and brings so much sorrow to this world. This is the poisoned gift of belief. Faith, on the other hand, requires strength to stay with hard emotions and dark personal truths that, if cultivated, can bring self-discovery and the humility required to see how we are complicit in our own suffering. But here's the thing. What am I supposed to have faith in? Without certainty, what holds me on the path in the Hindu forest of contemplation?

It is said that 90 percent of what we observe in the seemingly infinite night sky is not light but darkness. Not the darkness that terrifies us but the gateway to mystery. Not the shadows but the pregnant emptiness that is the primordial stew of creation. I'm confounded by that which I cannot see, but still there is this intuition, this gut feeling that in this darkness there is something magical and eternal.

Living as we do now, with the benefits of science in health care and in greatly reducing the power of religion in parts of the world to create war, has been one of the great triumphs of the last few hundred years. But this age of rationality has also seen some of the darkest acts in human history unfold with no religion in sight. There are more than a hundred million dead in the names of Communism, Nazism and Fascism, where cults of personality have offered us instead human gods with the power to decree who lives and who dies.

Yes, there is much darkness in the world, and much light, too. The chaos machine that is the daily news spins tales of death, mayhem and evil doing. A murder here, a bus over a cliff there, a car crash, a mad dash across the water that ends not in freedom but in drowning and death. Still, many millions of us walk our children to school each morning. We hug them, whether they want it or not, and say I love you to them as they run toward the jubilant energy of the playground. We are more than that which has gone wrong.

This is what I hold on to as I prepare to take a dive into the darkness of my own life. The regrets, the guilt, the shame for what I have done and not done. Those that I cannot forgive and those that cannot forgive me. Tough work, but I tell you what, I'll go first.

There was a good man who I worked with professionally. He was always kind to me and stayed in my corner when many others had abandoned me. I had reached the top of my profession, hosting and producing a big TV variety show, and he was there from the get-go as part of the crew. Later, after the show had failed terribly and my big chance had fizzled, most folks around me moved on. Turns out not many that arrive alongside your success want to marinate with you in your failures. But this man stayed right there with me, and as he rose through the ranks, he always found ways to invite me back into the glare of the lights.

In time, I had a big idea to produce a film for the public broadcaster. We worked it up the chain together. The network, it turned out, wasn't as thrilled with it as we were. They told me that it wasn't going to fly. In frustration, I asked if a new approach with a different partner would improve my chances. It was and still is something I am ashamed of doing. Shame, by the way, is not something that we should never feel. It's important to feel shame when we are wrong, and it is deeply wounding to be shamed when we are not. This time I was wrong. I was afraid that if this project failed then I myself might fade even deeper into the shadows. A place, I had been reading, that lots of folks would have been happy to see me go. In the end, the project went nowhere and shortly after I left the broadcaster. But something had happened. I had betrayed the support and loyalty of a good man. I apologized. Actually, I apologized every year for five years, but it was too late. We have not been friends since, and frankly I understand why. I am usually a loyal friend and can say that most of my friendships have lasted literally for decades. This one did not.

I have often wondered how many of these stories from my life will come to me as I lay dying. If I, like so many, will have buried them in the darkness of my soul. If I have guarded them from scrutiny, then perhaps dying will be the only place where the dam can burst and my deep regret can spill out. I realized that it is better to do this work before the final snows fall. Why wait till the cold chill of death is all that swirls around us?

So, here's the next question: How do we take on this freighted inventory of failure without succumbing to recrimination? A ritual seems to be in order. The prayer that is recited in the Jewish faith every Yom Kippur is an unrelenting litany of weaknesses. If we choose, we can move through the list with just a passing glance, not willing to dive deeper into the words we are saying.

We abuse, we betray, we are cruel.
We destroy, we embitter, we falsify.

As we recite each of these powerful indictments, we take our fist and tap the tough outer coating, the klipah surrounding our hearts. As we pound on our chests, we hope to break through that shell. As Leonard Cohen said, we need that crack in everything, that's where the light gets in. It is said that only through a broken heart can one find faith. Who can arrive there from strength, arrogance or anger. No one.

We gossip, we hate, we insult.
We jeer, we kill, we lie.

This all seems so harsh. Could I be that bad a person? Surely if any of this is true, I didn't really mean any harm.

We mock, we neglect, we oppress.
We pervert, we quarrel, we rebel.

What could be the point of such self-flagellation? Perhaps, as the late Rabbi Alan Lew said in his wonderful book on the Jewish High Holidays, *This Is Real and You Are Completely Unprepared*, as we say these words we might come to "realize that we have greatly overestimated our cleverness and our potency; we have overestimated the efficacy of our conscious behavior and we have underestimated the persistence and the depth of our destructive tendencies."

I know that what I'm throwing down here as an emotional and soul-searching gauntlet goes against our wise guy kill 'em all and throw in a quip culture, where the good/bad guy vigilante rides into town on something or other and blows the even badder guys away while muttering yippie ki-yah through cigarette-stained teeth, but the thing is, this work is much harder than that.

We steal, we transgress, we are unkind.
We are violent, we are wicked, we are xenophobic.
We yield to evil. We are zealots for bad causes.

My God what a bummer. Who wants to think that badly of themselves? But is it really thinking badly of yourself or humbling yourself to the thousand tiny cuts that make up the darker side of our hearts? This prayer is followed by the congregation asking forgiveness for the transgressions that have passed through their hearts and from their lips, either willingly or unwillingly over the past year. It's a life review that reads like a highlight reel of failings. It's obvious, at least to me, why when I look around the synagogue during the Viddui, as it's called, I see so many different levels of commitment to this ritual. Feelings of shame and a default to a position of reproach are always close at hand when we dare to take stock of our less-glorious moments.

But what is the alternative? Simply to live with these feelings and thoughts roiling beneath the surface of the social veneer we create in the hopes that others will think better of us than we do of ourselves? Perhaps we can relegate this work to the dream state. Leave the heavy lifting to our custom version of the passion play, the one that speaks in whispers around the fringes of our consciousness of forbidden thoughts and startling encounters. But as we age, perhaps we should muck about a bit in the cellar of regret.

One of my rabbis, Nadya Gross, a wonderful soul who has spent much time with the dying in her work as a spiritual director as well as cleric, has taken the Viddui and distilled it into three simple questions that we would be wise to answer. But unlike the traditional Viddui of the High Holidays, she begins with a positive accounting: Who I am; the accomplishments of which I am proudest; the relationships that are meaningful in my life.

By starting with a positive inventory, she has invited us though the front door of our lives. We get to talk about what we and others have recognized as the legacy that will unfold when memories are all that feed our loved ones.

Next: What have I left undone? What do I regret? This is where we do a little mud wrestling with our egos. We must consider the personal failings and deeds that we committed and of which we are deeply ashamed; as well we might be saying goodbye to dreams and aspirations that in our youth seemed within our grasp.

But I would caution that this is more than that. I believe that for many, autumn is the time in their lives when they can actually take up many forgotten aspirations. Those talents and yearnings that we shelved as we catered to family. Now, as we age up, perhaps there is a generosity that can flow from the idea that the time to work on oneself and for the common good is ripe. Regret can take the shape of guilt or yearning. Sometimes the recipe contains dollops of both.

Many speak of aging as ripening, despite the fact that part of us dreads that getting older will be filled with nothing but rot and decay. You know the thinking – you look down at your hand and noticed a raised blemish of some kind. What the hell is that? That wasn't there yesterday. Great, I better look that up. Raised blemish, translucent. This can't be good.

And we descend down the rabbit hole.

Now imagine if your worries were to come true, that the thing on your hand turned out to be a harbinger of something very serious. How well prepared are you to walk through that door? There is plenty out there that deals with cures, therapies, courses of treatment, and for the sake of the body that's good. But like so much else we live through, like birth and hormonal rites of passage, there is little that deals with the soul. As Stephen Jenkinson, the griefwalker and author of *Die Wise* says, we are concerned with curing but not so much with healing ourselves. So it goes with unresolved actions, relationships and lost opportunities. Yes, it is painful to stay with these feelings, but regret is not solely a room of shadows. If we work consciously – and that is the key – we can create a better story. Maybe even a better ending if it comes to that.

Jacob Marley in the Dickens classic *A Christmas Carol* shows us what happens when we forge a chain of regrets. I always loved the black-and-white film version starring Alastair Sim. Marley shows Scrooge the length of chain he is doomed to carry for eternity, to which Scrooge, determined to outrun his fate, reacts: "But it was only that you were a good man of business, Jacob." Upon which Marley's ghost cries out in anguish: "Business! Mankind was my business. [You have to say bus-a-ness to get the full effect.] The common welfare was my business."

We too carry our lengths of chain. The unkind word that leaves so many wounds in those we love. The casual infidelity that our yearning to be validated makes real. We are violent, we are unkind, we gossip. This is not all of who we are but wouldn't it be divine if we could sift through these transgressions and make restitution with those we have willingly or unwillingly offended. Often, we harden our hearts in the face of such a choice. "Well, I wouldn't have said those things if he/she hadn't started it. I've put up with a lot from them over the years." Hell, it feels good just writing that last bit. It's not me, it's the situation – or better yet, it's them. After all, a man can only take so much. I'm starting to feel like James Cagney, the classic Hollywood American gangster from the forties and fifties. Spunky, Irish and ready to bellow, "I've been framed, see, it was Flanagan. He's the bum who set me up!" I made up the last line, but you get the idea. What follows that scene is, of course, a flatfoot cop dragging Cagney into a waiting police car. Nobody's buying his story.

Henry David Thoreau once said, "Make the most of your

regrets; never smother your sorrow, but tend and cherish it till it come to have a separate and integral interest. To regret deeply is to live afresh."

The third question is: What do we want to be remembered for? What is our legacy? Here we can take a while to think about what we want people to say, like in that fantasy where we get to listen in at our memorial service, and better yet, to the conversations had at the reception afterwards. We hope people will say good things; we hope we will have deserved them. But legacy is not set in stone; we can still write new chapters in our story. We can start on any given day to do something that will make us proud and have other people in mind. Something for their good, for the betterment of friends and family. For whatever full-hearted endeavour we can think of.

Let's imagine that instead of fearing what a life review might bring – the dredging up of our mistakes, the past hurts and friendships that to this day lie in ruins – we tend to and cherish our failings, and build a living legacy. After all, even the act of doing so brings deep and meaningful value to what we have done, be it noble or beneath us.

In the Jewish tradition we have a process that engages us in a personal cleansing every new year. The lunar calendar we look to places Rosh Hashanah – the head of the year, the new year – in the fall. Usually in the Christian month of September. The harvest is in play and as the fields bend toward rest, we take stock of ourselves. During the process and between the celebration of the new year and Yom Kippur, we gather up our transgressions and the regret that they have brought us. We're to write them on pieces of paper and then go to a water source to toss them away as we ask forgiveness. It is called tachlit. Like so much in Jewish practice it's a process. We start with penance during the ten days of Rosh Hashanah, the true reckoning that finds us willing to take responsibility and make that which we would rather bury real. We have to decide for ourselves to be free of the burden of guilt.

Another piece of the Rosh Hashanah puzzle that prepares us for our personal reckoning on Yom Kippur is that a mitzvah, or good deed, is undertaken to seek out those that we may have offended and ask their forgiveness. I remember doing this once with someone in my neighbourhood who would often join me for dog walks in the park across the street. I had been flippant with him one day. He was going through a divorce and with it a radical change in lifestyle. He was sharing with me, and all I could do was answer him glibly before cutting the conversation short because I had something "important" to do. Or so I remember it. I felt bad the minute I left him. The feeling stayed with me and returned at the oddest moments as the year passed. So here we were, walking our dogs before Yom Kippur, and I stopped and said, "Look, a while back you were sharing something with me about adjusting to your new life after divorce. I didn't really honour what you were telling me. I just wanted to say that I'm sorry. That I should have been there for you and that I hope this year brings you some happiness and connection to your daughters in your new living arrangements. Anyway, I'm sorry."

He looked at me, a bit surprised. I'm sure he was trying to remember what on earth I was talking about. The conversation had clearly left more of a mark on me than on him. A smile broke across his face. "Don't worry about it," he said. "It's no big deal." We said our goodbyes a little while later, and as he walked away, he added, "Hey, Ralph. I really appreciate that you did that, but don't sweat it, it's all good."

So why bother?

Do I want to be trying to process and act on these pieces as I lay dying or would my life be better for acting on them now? By engaging in this process now we can move from a space filled with scores unsettled and wrongs un-righted to a much larger landscape of connection. A life that has more deeds and thoughts that have not been stopped mid-sentence, left hanging.

The story is told of a rabbi who says to his students that anyone who repents even one day before they die will be redeemed. But, Rabbi, they ask, how will we know what day that is? Exactly, says the rabbi. So, it's best we do it now.

Frankly I think that if I'm lucky enough to be even remotely lucid as I pass, I would regret it more if I had never taken stock, never made amends and finished those conversations that might have brought closure for myself and those I have travelled through life with. Whether or not they can, or choose not to, engage me in that process is not a deal breaker. I can speak directly to someone I have harmed in some way or I can write them a letter that I will never send.

Central to the process is to avoid the trap of self-pity and to instead take a deep, personal responsibility for what has come to pass. In doing so, we take our true and honest place in the narrative. Regret requires some form of relationship. This is not to say that we must seek out and mollify those who have done much to harm us in one way or another. It doesn't mean that we must resume relationships that have died for good reason, but it does mean that we take honest account of our part in their failure. Make no mistake, this is tricky work. What starts as an exercise in humility can end with self-congratulation and pity for the other guy.

I don't believe anyone who says they have no regrets. There is an arrogance in banishing regret from our narratives. It's as though the acknowledgement of egregious actions might leave us too vulnerable. It might encourage others to look for more of our failings in an effort to themselves prop up a false sense of superiority.

There is only one cure for the toxic effect that regret can and does have, and that is forgiveness. The American Buddhist psychology movement is led by people like Jack Kornfield, who tells the story of two former prisoners of war that meet years later:

> When the first one asks, "Have you forgiven your captors yet?" the second man answers, "No, never." "Well then," the first man replies, "they still have you in prison." For most people, the work of forgiveness is a process. Practicing forgiveness, we may go through stages of grief, rage, sorrow, fear and confusion. As we let ourself feel the pain we still hold, forgiveness comes as a relief, a release for our heart in the end. Forgiveness acknowledges that no matter how much we may have suffered, we will not put another human being out of our heart.

This, Kornfield admits, is easier said than done. In his own case he could forgive many, and at times even himself, but the greatest test of his Buddhist sense of compassion was in the life and death of his father. This was the man who had beaten Kornfield's mother. A father who left deep, traumatic scars on all those around him. Kornfield was able to witness his father in the latter's dying days, and in that time, because as a meditator and practitioner of a loving path he had been preparing for this witnessing his whole life, he was able to find it in his heart to forgive. "I sat with him over long days and late nights. He kept asking me to stay. Because I had sat with my own pain and fear in meditation, I was not afraid. Because I had sat in the charnel grounds and with others as they died, I was able to offer the steady presence he needed. By now I also knew enough not to blurt out that I loved him, but I also knew that he could feel that I did."

This is heavy lifting, and without the spiritual discipline provided by years of practise, perhaps Kornfield would have left the room, made excuses for why he couldn't make it that day or simply found himself acting out in passive-aggressive ways.

Canadian poet Al Purdy wrote a stunning poem, "On Being Human," about witnessing his gravely ill mother's final act of aging. How while distractedly visiting her she had seen through his façade of care and in that moment realized that, in fact, he didn't – care that is. "I thought you'd feel terrible," she said. She had fallen, and the decline and pain of what she must have known was coming had not moved her son. She was soon to die. Purdy would carry the shame and regret of that failed response into his art, into his life and soul:

> But I remember those last words
> list them first
> among the things I'm ashamed of.

Purdy does us a great favour in his mea culpa. He lets us know not that he is worse than us but that we are all stumbling, failing and human. That our best does not always surface when it is being called upon. If we are not preparing the ground for a better response then indeed it may not blossom when we need the flower of its wisdom the most.

I have always wondered what a life that included confession would have been like. Knowing, even while transgressing, that one can unburden themselves, that another human being can be the repository for one's sins and the conduit to their forgiveness. Clergy in the Catholic faith would no doubt say that they are not absolving people but that they are a conduit to the divine, a vessel that, when filled, spills over into the unconditional love that is for many the bosom of the Lord. Forgive me, Father, in our patriarchal constructions of God – if one can get past the notion that God is a thing then I suppose that thing must be relatable in some human form, be it a priest, a nun or Jesus himself.

Richard Rohr writes, "In Jesus, God was given a face and a heart. God became someone we could love." While God can be described as a moral force, as consciousness and as high vibrational energy, the truth is, we don't (or can't?) fall in love with abstractions. So God became a person "that we could hear, see with our eyes, look at, and touch with our hands" (1 John 1:1). The brilliant Jewish philosopher Emmanuel Levinas said the only thing that really converts people is "an encounter with the face of the other," something I think he learned from his own Hebrew scriptures.

I know that many absolutions are also directed through the feminine divine via the personage of Mary, so perhaps there are alternate pathways to the loving destination. Either way, I, as a Jew, have to go on a different journey.

The Harvest

What would be tragic is to die having felt that I never showed up in this life. – Parker Palmer

If you don't know of Parker Palmer, he is an American Quaker and social and spiritual activist, and certainly worth listening to and reading. He has shared, among other things, insights about aging and our sense of purpose. As he sees it, there has to be something that trumps effectiveness. Not that I'm arguing that utility isn't important. I'm looking instead at the intangibles that can transform work and bring a sense of purpose. Decency, an ethical base and institutional wisdom that can temper the rush to achieve.

Palmer asks us to do something very important on our

journey into the time of harvest. He wants us to take our gifts and marry them to the needs we see in the world around us. In the intersection of these things we can do service to those around us, leave a legacy and gain a new sense of purpose. Without purpose, without a "why," as we discussed when talking about Viktor Frankl, we cannot survive the "how" of life. Imagine that you are a lifelong bookkeeper. Your services are no longer required by the large company you worked for; they can outsource that now. That turn of events can drive you into isolation, even bitterness. But the gift you have for numbers and planning has not disappeared. In your community there is a worthy not-for-profit that can't afford a bookkeeping service. You believe in what they do. You don't want to work five days a week anymore. You get together and work out something that is not too onerous to either side. You have a reason to get up, and they have someone who can keep their books. Bingo – purpose.

As we open our eyes to the opportunities of aging, we can refine our aim and with a clear eye bring a new meaning to the autumn of our lives.

From Success to Significance

So how do we cross the bridge? What can we do to make sure that as we age, we refine our sense of purpose? Our aim as it were. After all, we are dealing with an entirely different set of circumstances than the ones that we were given as young people. Some of the answers to this may be found in a definition I was given around the idea of sin.

Instead of seeing it as self-flagellation, Jewish scholars say that sin is simply a lack of aim. Yes, aim. As we navigate this life, we must take the opportunity to look down the shaft of the arrows we loose and to the targets we strive to hit. Is the target the right one? Is our aim true? Have we spent time refining our technique, being mindful of what we are really hoping to achieve?

The Buddhists speak of living an unskilled or a skilled life.

We know when we are being unskillful – at least I do, most of the time. Sometimes it hits me while in the middle of giving one of my boys a hard time when I should be holding him in my arms, or when I'm being harsh in response to something my wife has said. Life can be seen through this lens as a craft. We can refine our technique and become better prepared for the cascade of events that inevitably face us on a daily basis. That moment that we lean on the car horn as someone cuts in front of us. Someone, for all we know, potentially desperate to get to their loved one's bedside, or simply trying to get home before their child goes to sleep. Or maybe they too have lost sight of the target, have neglected to refine their aim, just like us.

The conventional idea of sin is of little use to me if instead of feeling humility I find myself feeling shame. Shame too often is a dead end. To escape it is to act compulsively, wanting to avoid the burning sting that it provokes. But the idea of having a target that is true and developing the skill to hit it – not nail it, just hit it – gives me something proactive to work for. Something within my grasp.

The target. That's the tough one. What are we aiming for? If not success then what? I was speaking with a friend who has also been a financial guide for me for over thirty years. He asked me about the book I was writing. We spoke about success and significance as I was on my way out the door. He asked me to stay a minute longer, and to close the door if I wouldn't mind. I sat with him and he told me that he was in some ways stuck in his success, with no idea how to bridge to a life that offered anything different. Anything that he would call significant. First, we acknowledged that he has made a real difference in the lives of his clients over the years. That he has been a loving father and husband, and that all of that is worth embracing.

But when it came to finding a new target, one that could be his legacy, he was at a loss. I knew he wanted me to tell him something that might help, to give him guidance. But no lightning bolt came to me, nothing that could shine a light on his path. The work is personal. It starts in the Viddui with an inventory of who we have been, who we are and what we want to be remembered for.

Who do we love? What are we most proud of? What do we regret?

As we collect those thoughts, we can look at our target with a clearer eye, unclouded by buried feelings and deep regrets. But it's the last piece, the legacy bit, that can become the new target. The piece that is not about who we have been but who we may yet become.

In one of my men's Age-ing to Sage-ing workshops, I had mentioned that we spend much of our lives believing that we have to be heroes, leading the parade. But now, in our autumn, we have a chance to move to the sidewalk, if just a little bit, and from there cheer on the next generation. For some around the table this was a hard one to internalize. Difficult because it spoke to male identity and work. If I am not a doctor, what am I? There was talk of the dreaded word – "retirement" – and the notion that men, within a few years of retiring, just up and die. One man took up the challenge. He asked, "If I'm not what's on the business card, what can I say that I do? How do I stay in the parade in some way?" That's the work of building a legacy. Of paying it forward.

We can refine our aim to align with the changing winds of not decrepitude but age. We have the power to take back words like "old," "aging" and "senior" and make them into "mentor," "seeker," "elder" and "wisdom keeper." This is ours. We have earned every year of it and we know, more than most, that our time is limited.

The last piece of my Age-ing to Sage-ing workshops comes from the work of Reb Zalman Schachter-Shalomi. It is an address to the United Nations. I love what participants bring to this exercise. We often read them out loud, and the care and passion that goes into these speeches touches me every time. Whether it is about child poverty, the destruction of the coral reefs or the crisis of clean water in the world, the exercise can bring out passions in our elders that speak to the urgency with which these issues must be addressed. When you're in the autumn of life you become cognizant of the finite nature of this mortal moment. Life, human life, is now measured in decades at best if not years as we progress up the ladder of aging. Thoughts about what we leave behind come into focus.

I remember sitting in a meeting a few years back where the proposed completion of a strategic plan and its objectives was twenty-five years from the day of the meeting. Without thinking, I blurted out, "No, that's way too long." What I was thinking was, hey man, I'll be dead by then, we need to be doing something now. I'm not interested in going carbon neutral by 2050. First, the planet will be beyond human repair by then and, second, I want to see that happen now, because I know if we marshalled the resources and political will we could get it done actually, really done, by 2030.

Is it vain of me to think it matters because I could be around for that? Perhaps, but it is also something that age has gifted me – the realization that we can continue to kick the world's tragedies down the road and live unconsciously, or we can come together and make tomorrow into today. My awareness of the fact that my human life is but a blink in the eye of creation is real and may be a catalyst for renewing my purpose in the time allotted. The delusion of eternal life gave inspiration and passion to my younger self. But living for tomorrow may be our ruin. I want to fuel my elder years with the experience and cultivated wisdom that only elders can offer at the other end of life.

This time is not simply for taking inventory. It's a time for action.

What's the Plan?

Good question. In the second half of my professional career, I stumbled into the work of being an advisor. Working with political leaders, academic presidents and environmental groups. Like so much in my life, I didn't mean it, it just happened. This kind of work is best explained as flying at thirty thousand feet. It's not the operational excellence that is in demand so much as the lateral thinking mash-up of data, inspiration and the ability to identify what problem needs solving. In my capacity as an advisor, I tried to discern the desired destination of a problem, then would reverse-engineer back to the present moment to chart a path forward with timelines and deliverables.

Surprisingly, most organizations don't do this well. They are so consumed by the operational demands of the day that they don't think they have the time to "dream." If this sounds a lot like our daily lives, it's because it is.

***

We interrupt this book for an important message. Or, as they said in that nineties sitcom classic *Third Rock from the Sun*, "Incoming message from the Big Giant Head!" It would appear that I'm about to get whacked in the head again by some form of cancerous material. Not sure which one or how bad as I write this, but I'm hoping for another cranky old squamous cell carcinoma. I know it sounds exceedingly strange to hope for a cancer, but I know this one and the outcomes of having it are usually good. Might be worse, doubtful that it will just be benign. I know this because I just visited the doctor(s) about a cyst on my upper neck, and after an ultrasound and then a CT scan I found myself on the receiving end of not one but two needles right into the cyst. Yes, a needle biopsy. I did ask if it was going to hurt, and the doctor was kind enough to say, "Yes it will," before digging in.

I know I'm being glib but that's because I am honestly feeling the opposite – filled with dread and under attack. I had thought that cancer was something that I could refer to as a big fat teaching moment. A gift, as I have called it in these writings. I thought I had it all figured out, that I was one of the lucky ones. Now I've been thrown back into the pit. Uncertain, vulnerable and feeling angry. What is this about? Is what I actually said about vibrant aging and growing older just wishful thinking? Is it mostly about decrepitude?

Maybe all that I have been thinking and sharing with you about the autumn of life is just bullshit.

Like they say, "Everybody has a strategy until they get punched in the mouth." When I was a kid sitting on the rug in our apartment while my parents played canasta with their friends, I would overhear their conversations in Spanish. "Did you hear about Samuel?" "No, que paso?" "Un heart attack." "No. El pobre." Now it's my friends who bring stories of sickness and passing, but this time it's posted on Facebook and the comments in return are often well meaning but lacking substance. "So sad, thinking of you."

So I busy myself until the biopsy results are in, once again feeling helpless and worried that I will let my wife and children down. That I won't be able to calm my eleven-year-old as it seems only I can do. That my fourteen-year-old won't be able to spin hilarious stories that we build together like some sort of comedy Lego.

My older boys are finally settled, and like my father before me I will be unable to see them raise their children. Here's something: I'm not afraid that I am going to die. I'm just so bloody disappointed that I won't be there for those I love. I sometimes want to walk up to my wife, the love of my life, and say, "Look, you're still young, beautiful and so brilliant. You should leave me for this part of the journey and find someone younger. Remember, you're sixteen years younger than me. Go get a fifty-year-old. A good man. Let me do this journey into MRIs and needle biopsies by myself. I'll manage."

Full disclosure: What I usually tell her is "Listen, after I die, I seriously don't want you to find someone else. As a matter of fact, even though I will be buried, as is custom in the Jewish faith, I want you to get an urn, a decoy urn as it were. Put a big plaque on the front that just says 'Ralph' and place it on the mantel so that any potential suitors will look up and experience an immediate buzzkill."

Unfortunately, I have found no great wisdom or teachings

to back up my petty and absurd demand. Of course, what I'm really trying to say is that I want to be part of their lives. That I want to keep learning and sharing, that it's not fair that this life has limits. Why is it that purpose and legacy are best enjoyed by others, and that dying is the best way to pass that gift along?

It's so easy for me to say that we must die so that the cycle of creation can continue, but it's harder to fall asleep at night thinking that some doctor might enter a sterile examination room in a few days and tell me that they have a pretty good idea when that dying will be upon me.

***

Wait, this just in: It was a squamous cell carcinoma but it was successfully removed and no follow-up treatments were necessary. All right, let's get back to renewing our purpose

***

There are two ways to go about this in my experience. Renewing our purpose, that is. One needs to follow the other. First job is to do the work that we have been talking about, the work of cleaning the container. I emphasize this because without the clarity that comes with that work, we are prone to making the wrong decisions. We realize we are aging; we can be scared, which makes us hurry so as not to leave a void where fear prevails and panic sets in. Like we noticed earlier, men who lose a spouse later in life almost always find a new partner within months. Similarly, what we want to avoid is having a rebound purpose.

I made that mistake when I no longer had a full-time suit-and-tie job to go to every day. I thought I was going to be fine at first. I convinced myself that I was on a new path, but really I was just looking for more of the same. The pursuit left me fearful and unsatisfied. I went through a prolonged time of anxious dreams and deep worries that I was in many ways disappearing. I eventually got sick and tired of being sick and tired. I turned toward my spiritual life. Not as a desperate life-line but naturally, easily. I started taking my own advice.

This was my time to reap the harvest. My time to reap the rewards that forgiveness and reflection can bring.

Not That Kind of Rabbi

What did I do? All around me I could see that very few organizations were interested in hiring a sixty-four-year-old. So, like when I took up stand-up comedy, I realized that I had to take control of what I wanted to say and find a way to make it pay off – not in money but in claiming my voice, in not waiting for someone else to tell me what I could say and how I could say it. I launched a podcast called *Not That Kind of Rabbi*. The name came to me when I was on one of my Jewish retreats in the States. I was with a group of men and we were consciously sharing. Something men don't do very much of.

Frankly, most men have very small emotional vocabularies. Doing this work with them has become very important to me. We were talking and I mentioned that I have never stopped thinking about whether or not I should become ordained. "I keep thinking of whether or not I should become a rabbi," I told them. "Not that kind of rabbi, mind you, tending to a congregation, dealing with the politics of the role and seemingly never keeping everyone happy. No, a different kind of rabbi. More a spiritual companion with a great tool kit for helping people." One of the men, a fellow drummer and marketing man from Boston said, "Hey, that's it, you said earlier that you wanted to start a podcast. That's what you should call it. Not that kind of rabbi."

The drive home after the retreat takes about seven hours. By the time I walked through the door of my house two things were clear: the name of the podcast and the fact that I had to stop chasing who I had been.

I always remember when former senator and comedian Al Franken played the insipid New Age guru Stuart Smalley on *Saturday Night Live*. He soothed us with his weekly spiritual pablum in one episode, starting with something like, "I know I should be kinder to others, I should . . . Oh wait a minute," he almost whispered. "There I go should-ing all over myself again." That little bit of comedy has oddly helped me even though it's clearly parody. It's not about what I should do but what being here, right now, is calling me to be.

One of my guests, many of whom have taught me much in our conversations, was the East-meets-West musician Harry Manx. Somewhere in that interview I asked how he was doing at this stage in his life. We're roughly the same age. He said something that not many people can say with a straight face. He said that he was content and at peace. I asked him how he got to that treasured destination. He mentioned Advaita Vedānta – basically, accepting what is and being here, now.

I went downstairs after taping the interview, and there on my bookshelf was *A New Earth*, by Eckhart Tolle. I picked it up and started reading. Tolle talks about a true self. His philosophy draws on Buddhism and the same Hindu path of Advaita Vedānta that Harry had just spoken of. From there, I branched out to include the marvellous teachings of the Christian mystic Meister Eckhart. It is a curriculum that builds on the difficult notion of total presence. The difference between "I am Ralph Benmergui" and simply, beautifully, "I am."

The elder years give us a chance to contemplate, to take a measured step back, and in that process to let go of the story we have written so far. I never got that promotion. I could have made more money if I wasn't so stuck on living near my family. Why do I have such bad luck when it comes to my health?

Tolle and the pantheists of our time, people like Richard Rohr and Matthew Fox (though Rohr would probably reject this assignation), are preaching about the unity of everything. Tolle puts it this way: There are two ways to see the word "I." There is the deep I and the surface I. The surface I sees itself, you, as a separate entity often living in resistance to forces around it. The I that needs a name, status and all the things that we find so hard to let go of as we search for renewed purpose. The Ralph I tell everyone that I am.

Then there is the deep I. The I of being. Like the concept of Sabbath, there is a time for doing and a time for being. The deep I is an exploration of the self that is part of everything. The being that is made of stardust and will one day return to all that the universe ceaselessly creates. The deep I is the connection to the source. The search for the divine and the unknowable.

I know that this is not what your career coach is explicitly talking to you about as you cast about for calling or purpose, but it is the work that allows us to refine our aim. Do we really want, as elders, a life of one long shout of "I still got it"? Or can we gain humility and put a different lens on what it's like being closer to the end of this life than the beginning?

I am finding that it is better to realize that the only moment that matters is actually this one. Right now, as you read this. That for most of my life I have either been reacting to or scheming about what has already passed and what I want to have happen in the future.

Today we talk about mindfulness. It is a conversation that has been going on within religion for thousands of years. Meditation, contemplation – call it what you will.

As we age, making room for that practice will allow us to fear life less. The ego feeds off fear. We can and must fear death less if we are to make clear-eyed decisions about what we can do here and now.

I recently had a spiritual counselling client who was anticipating an upcoming knee replacement surgery. She was in an accident and had torn up her knee six years earlier. When we first spoke, it was clear that she felt victimized. It also became clear over time that she had been fed a narrative by her Holocaust-surviving parents, that life was not a positive experience. That they were basically, in the Jewish vernacular, shlamozzles who didn't deserve better. The knee injury was the fault of the dumb bus driver, the place that it had happened was Israel – and why in hell had she tried to live there anyways? She is a lovely, heartfelt woman, but her definition of life and the story she told herself every day to reinforce it were making her existence more unhappy than she deserved.

Now, in her late sixties, she was anticipating a surgery that struck fear in her heart. Sorrow, too, for thinking she shouldn't have suffered this long. Here you can see how the hammer of life shapes the hand. We began our work together by building a new narrative of loving kindness toward herself and gratitude for what she has. I asked her to write a list, a long list of things she loved about herself. I made it long on purpose – I wanted her to dig deep. She came up with fifteen lovely attributes, everything from loyalty to mentorship and beyond. I asked her to read them out loud to herself before she went to bed each night. She did, and when we met two weeks later she told me that in the repetition she felt that she was making friends with a different part of her being.

Then we started a list of gratitudes for recitation each morning. Slowly we were altering her story so that she could begin the journey toward the deeper I. Guided meditations followed, leading us to the spadework of presence. I say spadework because the non-thinking, just-being nature of the work is so foreign to our culture that we first have to check in with our internal mind police to get past the gate-keeping troll of our ego.

The work helped her do just that. And when she arrived at pre-op, she was able to return to the actual moment and not the one she feared was waiting for her down the hall in surgery. Post-operatively there was another challenge. As the analgesics wore off, there was pain in her knee. A lot of it. I offered her a different way of seeing it, relabelling the pain as sensation. Pain carries an enormous amount of emotional freight as a word. Mostly we don't think we deserve it. Why me? I want this to stop goddamnit!

She began to visualize the word "sensation." Sensation

arising and subsiding like a wave in the ocean. The purpose was to drain the anxiety and fear out of the moment; to breathe through it instead of resisting it. Even to look at sensation as a guide in her healing process. We have all kinds of drugs to kill pain, but we offer few salves for the spiritual challenge offered by something like knee replacement surgery. Mortality, vulnerability, loneliness, fear. Asking ourselves to increase consciousness in light of that seems counterintuitive. Rough translation, I'd rather not be here for this. Like Stephen Jenkinson says in *Die Wise*, we want to skip the dying part and just be dead. We would rather numb our way through an operation and its ensuing challenges. I know that has been my struggle.

My client found herself accepting her healing process with more kindness toward her aching knee. She got out of her own way and let herself slow down and heal. Before she would have skipped that healing part and just wanted to get on with it. Now if she needed to sleep for a few hours during the day or ice her knee while talking to a friend on the phone, that's what she did. This wasn't a battle of knee replacement; it was a loving process.

There are many situations in life when we prefer to be absent, emotionally, physically and spiritually. Confrontation, hard truths about relationships, feelings of regret and failures. Being present is warrior work, but I ask you: Wouldn't it be worth it to take that hill? To live life right now with all its beauty and, yes, suffering?

By being here and choosing to be conscious, many of my fears of the future have begun to melt away.

I introduced one more healing piece into my friend's spiritual recovery plan. When talking about the character trait of patience, Canadian Mussar practitioner Alan Morinis asks us to use meditation to create more space between what triggers us into impatience and what lights the fuse of anger. Through being present, being conscious, we can take the right action. "Truth and consciousness are preconditions to exercising free will. Only when the light of awareness is glowing brightly can we see the truth and choose to follow a course that is guided by our values and goals, not by our animal soul, instincts, emotional reactions and habits." That's what I'm trying to get at when I talk about cleaning the container before refocusing our efforts as the years roll on. I speak from a place of experience – as my reflexes and habits sent me flailing about, I found the choices I had made in the past were no longer suited to my new station in life. Basically, I had brought the wrong clothes on the trip into elderhood.

Morinis also writes about humility and gives us a continuum on which to chart that trait. Humility is in the centre of this continuum, with the extremes of self-debasement on one end and arrogance on the other. Like all other character traits, we can veer from one end of this spectrum to the other. The deciding factor on where we land is not force of will but the cultivation of a mindful presence.

Time for a caveat emptor. As the sacred tries to elbow its way back into our society – which prizes the material and the rational above all else – I see that there is little to no counterweight of mystery. Contemplation and stillness have fast become commodified as faux ingredients of everything from bath soaps and yoga mats to condo living. The Buddha has become a garden gnome. We need to re-sanctify these practices and enlist their profound power so that we can connect to where we stand and what calls to us.

I don't know if this helps you but it works for me when

I confront that odd piece of my journey toward finding true mindfulness. I have learned to let go of judgment and disappointment from time to time. In doing so, I have opened up to the meditative practices that suit me. No, I don't enjoy sitting in a lotus position for twenty minutes twice a day. Instead I play the djembe or the darbuka (African and Arabian drums). Am I a great drummer? Who cares, I'm not practising for a performance. I'm letting go and listening to what the drum is telling me. As soon as I try to control the flow that resonates as my hands hit the drum it all falls apart. I must surrender to what is. I listen to sacred music and chant the eastern European Jewish scat of the niggunim. I listen to the ambient genius of Brian Eno and as I walk, I take note of the monkey mind that has dragged me through forests, and I let it go as I take in everything around me. The miracle that I am a part of. I have come to accept that there is no right way to be, to do, to walk through this life if I am not coming from a place of authenticity. If I don't take the chance of being seen for who I am. That doesn't mean I give up the work of refinement. To be conscious is to challenge the myth of who I am and love the truth that lies beneath it in me and in all those around me.

Creating the *Not That Kind of Rabbi* podcast has made me realize how little we talk with people about our spiritual lives. I have interviewed politicians, musicians, poets and, in one instance, a happy capitalist whose world view left my chin on the floor. He believed, quite simply, that we're born, we live and then we die. That's it. He challenged me, asking if that was a problem for me. I replied that I preferred to not be so certain. That I enjoyed giving some space to the idea of mystery. He scoffed then added that climate change was nonsense, or should I say inevitable. The sun, according to him, had a broken thermostat and we were suffering the effects. Nothing we could do. I didn't take the bait. I wanted to hear him out. It did make me wonder if high capitalism is compatible with a reinvigorated spiritual society.

I spoke with Kathleen Wynne. She was the first openly gay premier of Ontario and the first woman leader in this province of 14 million. She spoke of life passages and the transition from being a maiden, a mother and to now wanting to reclaim the title of crone.

Poet Robert Priest talked of his year-long stay in a psychiatric ward for severe depression. His reluctant but grateful embrace of ECT – electroconvulsive therapy. The love of his wife, who came to see him almost every day and went home wondering if she would ever get her beloved back.

I have realized that we all have a spiritual story of our own, and that they manifest in different ways. Hockey broadcaster Tara Slone was brought up Buddhist in the highest per capita population of Buddhists in North America, the Shambhala group in Halifax, Nova Scotia. We didn't talk *Hometown Hockey*, a show she co-hosts, just Buddha. When it was over, she told me how happy it made her to leave the puck behind and speak from her heart.

The podcast is good medicine for me on my journey.

Do Not Cast Me Off in Old Age; When My Strength Fails, Do Not Forsake Me! – Psalm 71:9

As I write this, we are passing through a global pandemic that has claimed many lives and is changing us in many ways. But one sad truth that has been laid bare is how little we value our elders. In places like Texas and Alberta, politicians have informed us that the vast majority of deaths occurred in the aged, those at or close to eighty. A choice was given to us: get the economy going and let some old folks die, folks who were past their due date anyway, or shut it down and risk the livelihood of others.

The most acceptable "ism" of our time is ageism. As I have said and many others have pointed out, we know the price of everything and the value of nothing. We live in a death-phobic culture, and our elders remind us too much that death awaits. Yes, the process of getting older is a physical challenge, but it is also a spiritual one. It is a chance to reclaim our soulful existence. But our elders will remain invisible if we simply wait as a society for acknowledgement and respect for them to appear. If we truly respected our elders, we would demand an end to the warehousing of people as they age. No one would find themselves in a waiting room filled with loneliness and strangers on their way to a dusty, airless death. When I ask people to write out their obituaries, they never paint that picture for themselves. They envision dying peacefully at home, surrounded by love.

If we want to create Wisdom Councils that will assist us in making decisions infused with experience, context and passion for leaving behind a legacy for generations to follow, we will have to carve out a place for elders at the tables of power.

Right now, one of the most powerful voices in the campaign to stop the war on Mother Earth comes from a teenage girl. God love her but where are our elders? If we have received the gift of longer lives then is it not incumbent on us to reject the label of doddering old fools and engage with our communities in an effort to bring our spiritual gifts to bear?

When I was young, I saw religion as a weak-kneed insurance policy that those who feared dying paid into in hopes of a heavenly reward. I didn't need that reassurance.

Well, I'm older now and, yes, improved. I fear and I accept that my life, this human life, is finite. Thing is, I don't fear my so-called end; I fear hurting those I love with my passing. And I know that such sorrow is real and hopefully well earned.

I see religions as sources of profound wisdom, providing ritual tool kits to help people through the cycles of life. More importantly I have come to believe that without a spiritual life we have devolved into a place of arrogance. With our humility gone we have become rapacious and entitled. We have thrown God out. We look for a different type of certainty when facing the unknown. The kind that toxic men offer through law, order and the power of the mob.

God is a verb to me. A process of unceasing creative power. I have never pretended to fathom its depth. I never stop marvelling at its manifestations, the genius that is evident all around us on this silly little dirt ball of a planet in a minor galaxy surrounded by literally hundreds of millions of other galaxies.

I have tried to be honest about the lack of grace and sometimes dignity in my life. I have shared this with you because, as I said at the beginning of this book, this is not a rehearsal. The death of my father, his massive stroke three days before his official retirement with his bags already packed for a well-deserved holiday, a holiday that he never had, forever changed the geography of my life. We don't have to wait to go through the steps I have laid out in the process of reclaiming and making conscious our journey. We can do it all right now.

Contemplating our own death and bringing that truth out of the shadows, taking stock and asking forgiveness, writing our Vidduis – who do I love and what have I accomplished; what do I regret and what do I want to be remembered for. Writing a letter to those that we love and standing before the world to say: This is what I care about. This is a wrong I want to help right. Finding renewed purpose and standing proudly to say, I am. I am old and improved.

Epilogue

My eleven-year-old won't go to sleep. He can't. He has to keep reading *Diary of a Wimpy Kid*. At my age I shouldn't even know that this book exists. But I do. I'm tired, he's eleven, this probably won't go well.

"All right, enough with the book. Would you please stop getting up to turn on the hall light so you can keep reading? It was time for bed an hour ago."

"Okay," he says, in his little boy voice.

"All right, I love you. Good night."

How did I get here? Me, turning sixty-five, and him telling me the next day, "You're not a grumpy old man, you're not seventy yet. You're a grumpy middle man." Sad as it is, I'm willing to take the reprieve at face value.

I'm one of a growing cohort of men. Two marriages, two

sets of kids. Mine are thirty-four, thirty-one, fifteen and, as just mentioned, eleven, all boys. I have navigated the swampy and chaotic journey through adolescence with the first two, and now two more are on deck, growing hair in strange places. I find myself wondering: Will I have the juice to stare out the window on a Saturday night wondering why they still haven't come home, still haven't called?

Aren't I supposed to be spending my weekend mornings slowly reading the paper? Yes, I still read printed newspapers, and yes, I also surf digital platforms. Hell, I create content for them. In many ways I'm blessed. From my first son I have two granddaughters, and my second has a wonderful seven-year-old through his partner. I see the first brood when I can while my youngest sons remain a full-time job.

This is where I'm supposed to say I'm not complaining. But I like complaining, it takes the edge off. Frankly I think there's way too much of this stiff upper lip, keep your voice down, pull your socks up mentality floating around like a dark grey cloud above our heads.

At my age I'm told I'm supposed to be out playing golf, counting the days till my pension kicks in. Thing is, I hate golf, truly hate it, and the pension is more of a supplement than my ticket to heaven.

For me, the primary reason to stay alive is that I don't want my younger ones to have to deal with their dad leaving this mortal coil before they have grown into young men. It's quite the motivator. I'm always doing the math. "Well, if I last another thirteen years then he'll be twenty-eight and the little one will be twenty-four. Great, I got them through college, providing the planet hasn't gotten rid of us all by then."

As you can see, the conflict is real. I am entering the autumn of my life while at the same time continuing the summer's work of planting seeds and tending my growing garden.

That means still finding work and making decent money. Meanwhile I'll take the kids to laser tag, where they run around like chickens and sit amidst a battery of incredibly loud arcade games, holding onto their winnings and yelling, "Hey, kid, come over here and spend some of your parents' retirement nest egg."

This book is about the passage through our seasons. For me, and for so many others, the leaves have begun to fall. But isn't that where so much beauty lies? It's in that riot of colours – the fiery reds, brilliant yellows and copper-tinged leaves that give us one of the most beautiful gifts we have: the gift of cherishing and sharing our mortality. The gift of grace. This is not the age of surrender. This is the time to collect our gifts, and to offer them to a world in need of elders and their mentorship.

In the end, my eleven-year-old fell asleep. Just a few years ago he would crawl into our bed. He was all elbows and gnashing teeth. I hated it then, I miss it now. He loved to lie between us and feel the warmth of his mother's body as he slept. All that commotion made me grumpy. But still, looking at him now, content and asleep, makes this work of eldering all the more urgent. It's not just that I want to see him through to manhood. It's also for my sake. If I can find my wisdom while I cross this bridge into the autumn of my life, then the time we have together will be that much richer.

In writing this book I invite you to share this journey with me. Because we are all, as they say, just walking each other home.

Ralph Benmergui is best known as a TV and radio personality. First at the CBC for over twenty years and then at Jazz FM with his morning show *Benmergui in the Morning*. Born in Tangier, Morocco, Ralph and his family arrived in Canada in the late fifties, settling in Toronto. Ralph has had an eclectic career. Stand-up comic, singer in a band, national media, then government communications. Executive Advisor to the President at Sheridan College and along the way seeking out and becoming an ordained Spiritual Director.